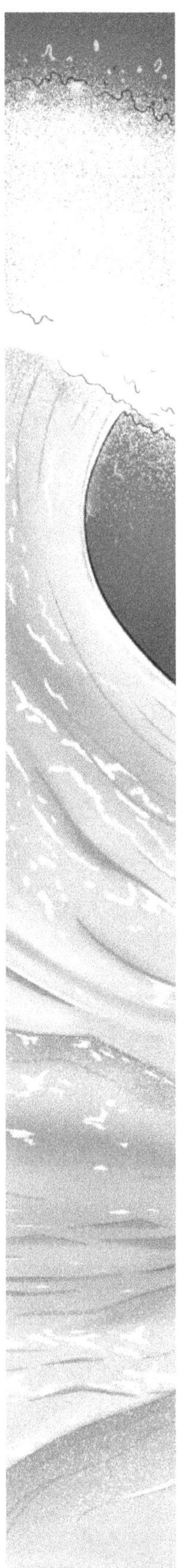

Rescue & Refreshment

Stormy Seas, Empty Goblets, & Jesus

by Ruth J. Leamy
illustrations by Lydia Leamy

... Let anyone who is thirsty come to me,
and let the one who believes in me drink.
As the scripture has said, "Out of the believer's heart
shall flow rivers of living water." (John 7:37-38)

In Memory of Red Christian
my teacher, mentor, & friend

Table of Contents

Chapter 1: Thirsty for Living Water

Water.
It's essential to human life.
It delights us in all-too-brief rain showers in the desert summer.
It fills our bottles and glasses and ice cube trays with refreshment.
It flows out of faucets and showers to cleanse us.
It bubbles in fountains and streams, bringing us joy and relaxation.
It calms us with the peaceful beauty of lakes and oceans.
But water isn't always friendly and soothing–
It can leave us cold and wet and shivering
when we get caught in a rainstorm.
Water causes great fear in stormy seas or devastating floods,
causing us to cry out for rescue.

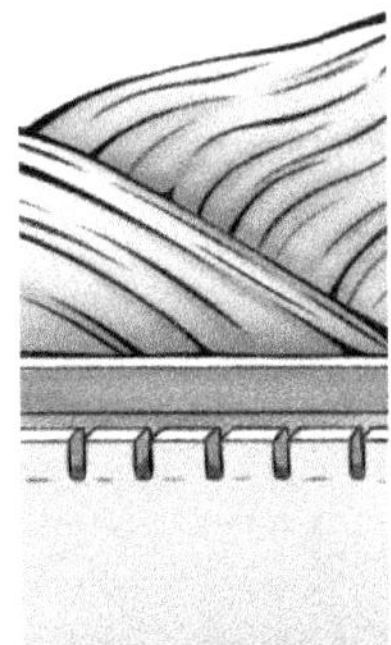

Reflect

What comes to your mind when you think of enjoying water?
A cool drink on a hot day? Floating around a pool? Gazing at the ocean?

Name a few dangerous situations involving water.

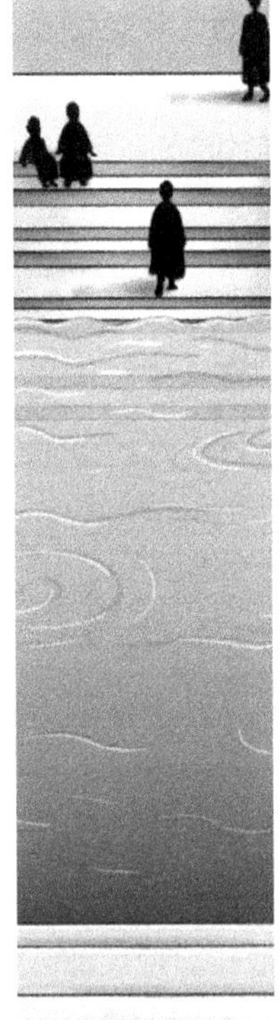

The earth is the Lord's and all that is in it,
the world, and those who live in it,
for he has founded it on the seas
and established it on the rivers. (Psalm 24:1–2)

As one of the necessities of life, it is no surprise that water is mentioned often in the Scriptures. This study will focus on Jesus' interactions with this fundamental element of life in the Gospels. We will see truths about his identity, power, and presence with us. We will enhance our study of these Gospel stories with complementary stories from other parts of the Bible.

Focus Gospel

We begin in John 7, reading the same passage from three versions as we ponder its message:

On the last day of the festival, the great day, while Jesus was standing there, he cried out, "Let anyone who is thirsty come to me, and let the one who believes in me drink. As the scripture has said, 'Out of the believer's heart shall flow rivers of living water.'" Now he said this about the Spirit, which believers in him were to receive; for as yet there was no Spirit, because Jesus was not yet glorified. (John 7:37-39 NRSV)

Now on the last and most important day of the feast, Jesus stood and called out [in a loud voice], "If anyone is thirsty, let him come to Me and drink! He who believes in Me [who adheres to, trusts in, and relies on Me], as the Scripture has said, 'From his innermost being will flow continually rivers of living water.'" But He was speaking of the [Holy] Spirit, whom those who believed in Him [as Savior] were to receive afterward. The Spirit had not yet been given, because Jesus was not yet glorified (raised to honor). (John 7:37-39 AMP)

On the final and climactic day of the Feast, Jesus took his stand. He cried out, "If anyone thirsts, let him come to me and drink. Rivers of living water will brim and spill out of the depths of anyone who believes in me this way, just as the Scripture says." (He said this in regard to the Spirit, whom those who believed in him were about to receive. The Spirit had not yet been given because Jesus had not yet been glorified.) (John 7:37-39 Message)

To understand this passage, we need to define three things: the feast, the living water, and what Jesus meant by "thirsty."

The Feast

Which festival or feast was being celebrated in the Scriptures we just read? Earlier in John 7, the Apostle John said that Jesus was celebrating the Festival of Booths or Tabernacles. This Jewish celebration involved traveling to Jerusalem and living in little booths or shelters for a few days to remember the nation's wilderness wanderings centuries earlier.

One of the events of this feast was a water-drawing ceremony. A priest would take water from the Pool of Siloam and lead a procession to the Temple. There, he would pour out the water on the altar. Everyone would recite Isaiah 12:3: "With joy you will draw water from the wells of salvation."[1]

This ritual recalled several Old Testament passages which promised a time of joy when rivers of living water would flow from the temple and the nation of Israel would be restored. (Ezekiel 47:1-2, Zechariah 14:8)

Living Water

What do the Biblical authors mean by "living water"? The Hebrew phrase used in the Old Testament (*mayim chaim*) describes fresh water in the form of a natural spring or falling rain. This phrase is used as a contrast to water that is stored in a cistern or carried from a well. It speaks of clean water that is drinkable, not seawater. Because ancient people saw this living water as water received directly from God, the phrase was also associated with the presence of God.[2]

When Jesus alluded to the promises of living water, he proclaimed that those who believed in him would experience living water that would flow not from the temple building, but from their own innermost being. John further explained that Jesus was speaking of the Holy Spirit. Perhaps some of the listeners remembered a promise from Isaiah:

For I will pour water on the thirsty land, and streams on the dry ground;
I will pour my spirit upon your descendants,
and my blessing on your offspring. (Isaiah 44:3 NRSV)

Reflect

Look back at your example of how you enjoy water. Maybe it brings you peace or refreshment or joy. Think about how the Spirit of God might bring you similar benefits.

Now consider your example of a dangerous watery situation. Think about how the Holy Spirit can provide a rescue from dangerous life situations.

Thirsty

Look at Jesus' statement again.

Let anyone who is thirsty come to me, and let the one who believes in me drink.
As the scripture has said, Out of the believer's heart shall flow rivers of living water.
(John 7:37–38)

What does the word "thirsty" mean here? We use the word when we crave the life-giving refreshment of water, the comfort of a cup of tea, or the eye-opening benefits of coffee. My concordance explains this word in John 7 by saying that thirsty people "painfully feel their want of, and eagerly long for, those things by which the soul is refreshed, supported, strengthened."[3]

Jesus was talking about a soul thirst–a deep need that only God can satisfy. We long to know that God is with us. We are thirsty for his comfort and encouragement, his rescue and refreshment.

When Jesus promises that the Spirit will give us rivers of living water, he assures us that our deep thirst can be satisfied by him. We don't have to travel to a temple or a church or a holy sight every time we want to meet him, because his Spirit dwells within us. We can express all our unmet longings to him and look to him to satisfy all our deepest needs.

I have added bold print to some of the selections of Scripture we read in this study, so that it can be read responsively within a group. (The leader reads the regular print, while the group responds with the bolder print sections.)

O God, you are my God,
I seek you, my soul thirsts for you;
my flesh faints for you,
as in a dry and weary land where there is no water. *(Psalm 63:1)*
I remember the days of old;
I think about all your deeds;
I meditate on the works of your hands.
I stretch out my hands to you;
my soul thirsts for you like a parched land... *(Psalm 143:5–6)*
For with you is the fountain of life;
in your light we see light. (Psalm 36:9)

With joy you will draw water from the wells of salvation.
And you will say in that day:
Give thanks to the Lord, call on his name;
make known his deeds among the nations;
proclaim that his name is exalted. (Isaiah 12:3 NRSV)

The Psalmist says that God is the fountain of life, the spring from which life flows, the satisfier of our soul thirst. Isaiah speaks of joyfully drawing water from the wells of salvation. (In the Old Testament, the word "salvation" refers to deliverance, rescue, or prosperity.[4]) These poetic statements speak of our longings as well as the source of true soul satisfaction.

But another Old Testament author reminds us that the people of God have not always turned to him as their source of life and deliverance:

For my people have committed two evils:
they have forsaken me,
the fountain of living water,
and dug out cisterns for themselves,
cracked cisterns that can hold no water. (Jeremiah 2:13 NRSV)

This is a powerful illustration. Imagine being near a fountain of fresh bubbling clear water, and choosing to turn your back on it and dig your own well–a poorly constructed cistern that will never hold water.

Reflect

How might we ignore God's presence and choose to satisfy our thirst from other sources?

What stories of Jesus can you think of that involve water or are set near a body of water?

Overflowing Truth

When we learn the truth about God and how much he loves each of us, this truth will overflow into our attitudes and actions. In each chapter, the section labeled "Overflowing Truth" looks at a simple truth that is demonstrated in the Focus Gospel–a simple truth that can change our lives.

In this chapter, I see God's attitude to thirsty people: he offers us refreshment. He is the only source of soul satisfaction.

My soul thirsts for God, for the living God.
When shall I come and behold the face of God? (Psalm 42:2)
Blessed are those who hunger and thirst for righteousness,
for they will be filled. (Matthew 5:6)
...Let anyone who is thirsty come to me,
and let the one who believes in me drink... (John 7:37-39)
It is done! I am the Alpha and the Omega,
the Beginning and the End.
To the thirsty I will give water as a gift
from the spring of the water of life. (Revelation 21:6)

Closing Prayer

As you read the selection from Psalm 107 below, ask the Lord to satisfy your soul's thirst.

Some wandered in desert wastes,
finding no way to an inhabited town;
hungry and thirsty,
their soul fainted within them.
Then they cried to the Lord in their trouble,
and he delivered them from their distress;
he led them by a straight way,
until they reached an inhabited town.
Let them thank the Lord for his steadfast love,
for his wonderful works to humankind.
For he satisfies the thirsty,
and the hungry he fills with good things. (Psalm 107:4-9)

~Notes~

Beside Still Waters

a personal time of meditation and prayer

At the end of each chapter, I have inserted an optional page titled "Beside Still Waters." This is a page for anyone who wants to soak in the truth of the Scriptures in solitude, while talking with Jesus about what you are reading.

To see the context of our Focus Gospel in this chapter, read the entire chapter of John 7. Check out the section labeled "Meditation Methods" in the Appendix on page 100. You may find that one of these methods will help you spend a little time with the Scriptures. (I suggest Method 1 for this chapter.)

Think about how we defined "thirsty" in this chapter and consider where you are in your spiritual journey. Are you

thirsty for peace? thirsty for joy?
seeking refreshment?
needing to be rescued from a storm?
soaking up all the spiritual nourishment you can find?

End your time in prayer. Talk to the Lord about your need for refreshment or rescue.

The Lord is my shepherd; I shall not want.
He makes me lie down in green pastures;
he leads me beside still waters;
he restores my soul. (Psalm 23:1–3)

~Notes~

Chapter 2: God's Beloved at the Jordan River

Reflect

Imagine that you are standing on the banks of a river, about to step into the water to be baptized. What do you think you might be feeling? Consider your physical senses as well as your emotions.

Gospel Focus

The Jordan River was a significant feature in Isreal's geography as well as its history. In the Old Testament book of Joshua, the Israelites crossed the Jordan into their Promised Land, entering a new chapter in their national life. In the Gospels, we read about Jesus beginning his public ministry at the Jordan River. Here is the account in the Gospel of Matthew:

> *Then Jesus came from Galilee to John at the Jordan, to be baptized by him. John would have prevented him, saying, "I need to be baptized by you, and do you come to me?"*
>
> *But Jesus answered him, "Let it be so now; for it is proper for us in this way to fulfill all righteousness." Then he consented.*
>
> *And when Jesus had been baptized, just as he came up from the water, suddenly the heavens were opened to him and he saw the Spirit of God descending like a dove and alighting on him. And a voice from heaven said, "This is my Son, the Beloved, with whom I am well pleased." (Matthew 3:13-17)*

At this time in Jewish religious culture, baptism was a ritual for proselytes (non-Jews who adopted the Jewish faith).[1] Thus, when John the Baptist urges everyone, even deeply religious citizens, to repent and be baptized, it is a new and puzzling concept that threatens the religious status quo. John is announcing a new era: the era of the Messiah's ministry. In the Gospel of John, we have a few more words from John the Baptist:

> *The next day he saw Jesus coming toward him and declared, "Here is the Lamb of God who takes away the sin of the world! This is he of whom I said, 'After me comes a man who ranks ahead of me because he was before me.' I myself did not know him, but I came baptizing with water for this reason, that he might be revealed to Israel." And John testified, "I saw the Spirit descending from heaven like a dove, and it remained on him. I myself did not know him, but the one who sent me to baptize with water said to me, 'He on whom you see the Spirit descend and remain is the one who baptizes with the Holy Spirit.' And I myself have seen and have testified that this is the Chosen One." (John 1:29-34)*

Reflect

For years John the Baptist has been aware that he will present the Messiah to the nation. Here he is at the Jordan River, baptizing repentant people when he suddenly realizes that he has just baptized the Messiah. What do you think he feels and thinks?

God's Chosen One, the Messiah, came to John to be baptized. John said, "I baptize with water those who repent of their sins and turn to God." (Matthew 3:11 NLT) It seems shocking to me that Jesus, the perfect Son of God, chooses to participate in John's baptism ceremony that expresses repentance. In doing so, he aligns himself with sinners–not the religious leaders who were critical of (and threatened by) John the Baptist. As he does this, Jesus demonstrates his willingness to be one of us and eventually to carry the burden of sin for all of us.

The Gospels give us a glimpse of all three members of the Trinity present at Jesus' baptism. As Jesus participates in this ritual, God the Father speaks from heaven, identifying Jesus as his beloved. The Spirit makes his presence visible. It is a beautiful beginning to Jesus' public ministry.

Overflowing Truth

As we consider Jesus and his baptism, we can ponder the fact that God's beloved son became one of us so that we too can become the beloved children of God.

> *..."This is my dearly loved Son, who brings me great joy." (Matthew 3:17 NLT)*
> *For our sake God made the one who knew no sin to be sin,*
> *so that in him we might become the righteousness of God. (2 Corinthians 5:21)*
> ***For God made Christ, who never sinned, to be the offering for our sin,***
> ***so that we could be made right with God through Christ.*** *(2 Corinthians 5:21 NLT)*
> *The steadfast love of the Lord never ceases,*
> *his mercies never come to an end;*
> ***they are new every morning;***
> ***great is your faithfulness.*** *(Lamentations 3:22-23)*
> *For God so loved the world that he gave his only Son,*
> *so that everyone who believes in him*
> *may not perish but may have eternal life. (John 3:16)*
> ***See what love the Father has given us,***
> ***that we should be called children of God;***
> ***and that is what we are.*** *(I John 3:1)*
> *For the Father himself loves you,*
> *because you have loved me*
> *and have believed that I came from God. (John 16:27)*

Reflect

How does knowing that you are God's beloved change your sense of identity or your self-worth?

How does knowing that you are God's beloved change your actions?

Another Story of Baptism

In each of the remaining chapters of this study, I have chosen a Scripture passage to supplement or complement the Gospel Focus that begins the chapter. For this chapter, I chose a baptism story from the book of Acts.

> *Then an angel of the Lord said to Philip, "Get up and go toward the south to the road that goes down from Jerusalem to Gaza." (This is a wilderness road.) So he got up and went. Now there was an Ethiopian eunuch, a court official of the Candace, queen of the Ethiopians, in charge of her entire treasury. He had come to Jerusalem to worship and was returning home; seated in his chariot, he was reading the prophet Isaiah.* (Acts 8:26-28)

Studying this passage requires us to answer a few questions. Firstly, what is meant in this context by the word "eunuch?" In the ancient Middle East, many rulers wanted their officials to be focused on their jobs and undistracted by women. Castration seems a rather serious step to take, but ancient rulers often held absolute power over their citizens. As time went on, the word "eunuch" came to mean a man in service to a ruler.[2] Thus, when we read about this Ethiopian eunuch, we know that he is an important official in his country, but he may or may not be capable of fathering a child.

The next question is, "what did the author mean by "Ethiopia"? In the Greek language of the time, the word for "Ethiopia" could mean anywhere south of Egypt. My study resources do not agree on exactly which kingdom of Africa this man came from, but they do agree that "Candace" or "Kandake" was a hereditary term for a queen or the king's mother.

This brings up our next questions: why was an African man traveling to Jerusalem to worship God? How did he know about the Jewish God? To answer these questions, we need to consider Old Testament history. Powerful nations conquered segments of Israel several times, and every conquest resulted in the relocation of Jewish people. Some of these displaced people ended up in Africa. Thus, the Ethiopian eunuch may have been a man of mixed heritage descended from relocated Jews. Alternatively, he may have heard about the Jewish faith from the descendants of displaced Jews.

One more question about this man: was he welcomed into the temple to worship in Jerusalem? The answer is yes, but in a limited way. The temple contained four courts: the Court of the Gentiles, the Court of Women, the Court of Men, and the Court of Priests. Foreigners were only welcome in the outer court–the Court of the Gentiles. Thus, most of the temple areas were off-limits to him.

During his travels through Israel, this man must have bought a scroll that contained a prophecy by Isaiah. He may have heard a few rumors about Jesus. Perhaps he wanted to check out some of the Scriptures and prophecies for himself.

As we move on in the story, we meet another character: Philip. In Acts 6, the early church chose seven deacons to oversee charitable distributions. One of these men was Stephen, and another was Philip. Stephen was the first martyr, and after his execution, a wave of persecution swept some of the early church leaders to other locations. Philip moved to Samaria. There he found a receptive audience and became a popular preacher and miracle

worker. Yet the Lord interrupts Philip's work to take him out of town to meet and witness to one man.

> *Then the Spirit said to Philip, "Go over to this chariot and join it."*
> *So Philip ran up to it and heard him reading the prophet Isaiah. He asked, "Do you understand what you are reading?"*
> *He replied, "How can I, unless someone guides me?" And he invited Philip to get in and sit beside him.*
> *Now the passage of the scripture that he was reading was this: "Like a sheep he was led to the slaughter, and like a lamb silent before its shearer, so he does not open his mouth. In his humiliation justice was denied him. Who can describe his generation? For his life is taken away from the earth."*
> *The eunuch asked Philip, "About whom, may I ask you, does the prophet say this, about himself or about someone else?"*
> *Then Philip began to speak, and starting with this scripture, he proclaimed to him the good news about Jesus.*
> *As they were going along the road, they came to some water; and the eunuch said, "Look, here is water! What is to prevent me from being baptized?" He commanded the chariot to stop, and both of them, Philip and the eunuch, went down into the water, and Philip baptized him.*
> *When they came up out of the water, the Spirit of the Lord snatched Philip away; the eunuch saw him no more, and went on his way rejoicing.*
> *But Philip found himself at Azotus, and as he was passing through the region, he proclaimed the good news to all the towns until he came to Caesarea.*
> *(Acts 8:29-40)*

At the Lord's instruction, Philip walks alongside the chariot (Acts 8:29 NLT). The chariot must be moving slowly (or Philip is walking quickly) because he can hear the Ethiopian reading aloud from a scroll. At the Ethiopian's invitation, Philip joins him and begins to discuss the Scriptures.

The Ethiopian responds to the good news with such immediate faith that he asks to be baptized at once. Unlike the worship he experienced in Jerusalem, there is no exclusion in this Good News about Jesus.

Church historians disagree about whether this man had a significant effect when he returned home. Some credit him with beginning the Christian church in Ethiopia.

I think the most important thing we can learn from this man is simply his inclusion in the stories of the early church. The Scriptures show us without a doubt that we are all welcomed into the Christian faith. None of us are excluded. The God who calls us beloved is inviting each one of us to draw near to him in faith.

Reflect

As you read the following Scriptures, consider what they are telling you about God. What is his character? What is his attitude towards us? (Throughout this

study, when I ask this question, you can look for descriptions of any or all members of the Trinity: Father, Son, and Holy Spirit.)

> *The Lord is not slow about his promise, as some think of slowness,*
> *but is patient with you, not wanting any to perish,*
> *but all to come to repentance. (2 Peter 3:9)*
> ***I truly understand that God shows no partiality,***
> ***but in every nation anyone who fears him***
> ***and does what is right is acceptable to him.*** *(Acts 10:34–35)*
> *For the grace of God has been revealed,*
> *bringing salvation to all people. (Titus 2:11 NLT)*
> ***For I am convinced that neither death, nor life, nor angels, nor rulers,***
> ***nor things present, nor things to come, nor powers,***
> ***nor height, nor depth, nor anything else in all creation,***
> ***will be able to separate us from the love of God in Christ Jesus our Lord.***
> *(Romans 8:38–39)*
> *...God's love has been poured into our hearts through the Holy Spirit*
> *that has been given to us. (Romans 5:5)*
> ***Therefore, since we have been made right in God's sight by faith,***
> ***we have peace with God because of what***
> ***Jesus Christ our Lord has done for us.***
> *Because of our faith, Christ has brought us*
> *into this place of undeserved privilege where we now stand,*
> *and we confidently and joyfully look forward to sharing God's glory.*
> *(Romans 5:1–2 NLT)*

Closing Prayer

Give ear to my words, O Lord;
give heed to my sighing.
Listen to the sound of my cry,
my King and my God,
for to you I pray.
O Lord, in the morning you hear my voice;
in the morning I plead my case to you, and watch...
I, through the abundance of your steadfast love,
will enter your house,
I will bow down toward your holy temple in awe of you... (Psalm 5:1–3, 7)
The Lord is my shepherd; I shall not want.
He makes me lie down in green pastures;
he leads me beside still waters;
he restores my soul. (Psalm 23:1–3)

~Notes~

Beside Still Waters

a personal time of meditation and prayer

Read Matthew 3 and John 1 to put the stories of Jesus' baptism into context. Check out the Meditation Methods on page 100 for ideas on reading and responding to these Scriptures. You might find Method #4 (Imagine the Scene) to be useful.

Think of someone you know who may feel excluded by religious people. Pray that they will hear God's invitation to accept his love.

End your time of reflection by thanking God for making you his beloved.

> *How precious is your steadfast love, O God!*
> *All people may take refuge in the shadow of your wings.*
> *They feast on the abundance of your house,*
> *and you give them drink from the river of your delights.*
> *For with you is the fountain of life;*
> *in your light we see light.* (Psalm 36:7–9)

~Notes~

Chapter 3: Filling the Goblets at Cana

Reflect

What is your favorite part of a celebration? Enjoying the food? Getting together with friends and family? Taking a break from your everyday routine?

Gospel Focus

In John 1, Jesus begins gathering the followers who will become the famous twelve, beginning with Andrew, Peter, Philip, and Nathanael. In John 2, this group of men is attending a celebration.

> *On the third day there was a wedding in Cana of Galilee, and the mother of Jesus was there. Jesus and his disciples had also been invited to the wedding. (John 2:1-2)*

We are not told whose wedding this is, but some Bible scholars have speculated that it might be the author John's wedding. In the book of John, he never refers to himself by name, so it would fit his writing style to write about his own wedding in this anonymous way. Interestingly, this event is recorded only in John, not in the other Gospels.

As we read the story, we see that Jesus' mother is aware of the behind-the-scenes situation, and she has a bit of influence over the servants at this house. Further reading in the gospels reveals that John is probably Jesus' cousin, so it makes sense that Mary is a familiar member of the groom's family or extended family.

> *When the wine gave out, the mother of Jesus said to him, "They have no wine." (John 2:3)*

Jewish weddings at this time in history could last for a week. As you can imagine, the hosts would need to purchase a large quantity of food and drinks. Running out of wine during the feast was a big embarrassment to the host and a discouraging start to a new marriage.

"They have no wine," Mary tells Jesus. She does not ask for help in any specific way. She simply lets Jesus know that there is a problem.

> *And Jesus said to her, "Woman, what concern is that to me and to you? My hour has not yet come." (John 2:4)*

Does Jesus' reply seem abrupt or a little rude? He calls her "woman" (a respectful word similar to our English words "ma'am" or "Mrs") instead of "mother."[1] He is beginning a ministry in which he will gather a new family around him, a family of assorted people from all walks of life. Mary, although always precious to him, will share Jesus with this new family.

Jesus tells her that his hour has not yet come. Perhaps he feels that it is not yet time to do a spectacular attention-getting miracle. He is working on a holy schedule now, and it will not always be the schedule anyone expects him to keep. The Amplified version expands on Jesus' statement:

> *Jesus said to her, "[Dear] woman, what is that to you and to Me? My time [to act and to be revealed] has not yet come." (John 2:4 AMP)*

Somehow after hearing those words, Mary knows that Jesus will do something about this problem. Notice her instructions to the servants:

> *His mother said to the servants, "Do whatever he tells you."*
>
> *Now standing there were six stone water jars for the Jewish rites of purification, each holding twenty or thirty gallons. Jesus said to them, "Fill the jars with water." And they filled them up to the brim. He said to them, "Now draw some out, and take it to the person in charge of the banquet." So they took it.*
>
> *When the person in charge tasted the water that had become wine and did not know where it came from (though the servants who had drawn the water knew), that person called the bridegroom and said to him, "Everyone serves the good wine first and then the inferior wine after the guests have become drunk. But you have kept the good wine until now."*
>
> *Jesus did this, the first of his signs, in Cana of Galilee and revealed his glory, and his disciples believed in him. (John 2:5-11)*

In these short verses, Jesus performs a quiet miracle. He responds to his mother, he assists the hosts of the wedding, but he still keeps a low profile. Only the servants and the disciples are aware that the water has turned to wine. John says that this event revealed Jesus' glory.

Reflect

Imagine you are the servant who is taking a goblet of the water-now-wine to the person in charge. What are you thinking and feeling?

Did you notice the reason the water jars were at the wedding?

John tells us that this is the first of Jesus' signs or miracles and that it led his followers to believe in him. What do you think they learned about Jesus from this event?

This story gives me such a beautiful portrait of Jesus. I love to think of him doing his first miracle at a party, keeping the celebration going, and enjoying the event with his friends. How amazing to think of the Creator living on earth as a human, enjoying the fruits and foods that he created! It also shows me that the disciples knew Jesus as:

- a man who is active in social activities
- a man who cares enough about his friends or relatives (who were hosting the wedding) to solve their problem
- a man who changes the water that was set aside for a religious ritual into a beverage for a party
- a man you can take your troubles to, as Mary did

Overflowing Truth

Mary's actions in this story are admirable. She doesn't spell out every detail of what she wants Jesus to do. She simply tells him about this issue and then takes the practical step of telling the servants to follow his instructions. What a beautiful example of taking our needs to the Lord in prayer and trusting him to handle them, while not neglecting the small practical actions we can take.

As you read the Scriptures below, look for God's promises and instructions to us.

God is our refuge and strength,
a very present help in trouble. (Psalm 46:1)
Call on me in the day of trouble;
I will deliver you,
and you shall glorify me. *(Psalm 50:15)*
...Indeed, you note trouble and grief,
that you may take it into your hands;
the helpless commit themselves to you;
you have been the helper of the orphan. (Psalm 10:14)
Do not be anxious about anything,
but in everything by prayer and supplication with thanksgiving
let your requests be made known to God. *(Philippians 4:6)*

Reflect

What promises did you read in the Scriptures above?

What instructions do these Scriptures give you?

Purifying Water at Marah

Our supplementary story this week is an Old Testament passage about the Lord solving a water crisis. The location of this event (Marah) comes from the same root word as the name "Mary." They both mean "bitter."

> *Then Moses ordered Israel to set out from the Red Sea, and they went into the wilderness of Shur. They went three days in the wilderness and found no water. When they came to Marah, they could not drink the water of Marah because it was bitter. That is why it was called Marah. And the people complained against Moses, saying, "What shall we drink?" He cried out to the Lord, and the Lord showed him a piece of wood; he threw it into the water, and the water became sweet... (Exodus 15:22-25)*

The Israelites have just experienced a miraculous deliverance at the Red Sea. Now they are trudging through the wilderness and facing a new difficulty. They have been without water to drink for three days.

As a desert dweller myself, I know how quickly one becomes thirsty if one is outside on a hot day, so I have sympathy for the crowd of Israelites. It's hard to ignore thirst, and three days without water must have seemed unending.

When they finally reach an oasis, they find that its longed-for water is too alkaline or too salty to drink. What a disappointment!

But unlike Mary in the story we just read, these people do not take their problem to God. Instead, they complain to their leader, Moses.

Moses did know where to seek a solution. God told him about some wood (perhaps a specific tree species) that could adjust the water. Imagine the relief the people felt.

Reflect

What do you think is the difference between stating an issue and complaining about it?

When confronted with a problem, how is it helpful to remember past situations where God answered your prayers and guided you through the troubled time?

As you read the Scriptures below, listen for God's comfort and reassurance that he will answer when you bring your concerns to him.

When the poor and needy seek water,
and there is none,
and their tongue is parched with thirst,
I the Lord will answer them,
I the God of Israel will not forsake them.
I will open rivers on the bare heights
and fountains in the midst of the valleys;
I will make the wilderness a pool of water
and the dry land springs of water. *(Isaiah 41:16–18)*
I will sing of your steadfast love, O Lord, forever;
with my mouth I will proclaim your faithfulness to all generations.
I declare that your steadfast love is established forever;
your faithfulness is as firm as the heavens. *(Psalm 89:1–2)*
You prepare a table before me
in the presence of my enemies;
you anoint my head with oil;
my cup overflows.
Surely goodness and mercy shall follow me
all the days of my life,
and I shall dwell in the house of the Lord
my whole life long. *(Psalm 23:5–6)*

Reflect

How would you summarize the lessons contained in the Scriptures we read today?
Did they show you something about the character of God?
Did they call you to action or prayer?

Closing Prayer

Lord,
today I bring you my thirsts, my longings, my needs.
I trust your goodness and your mercy
to bring springs of comfort and joy
into the desert places of my life.

~Notes~

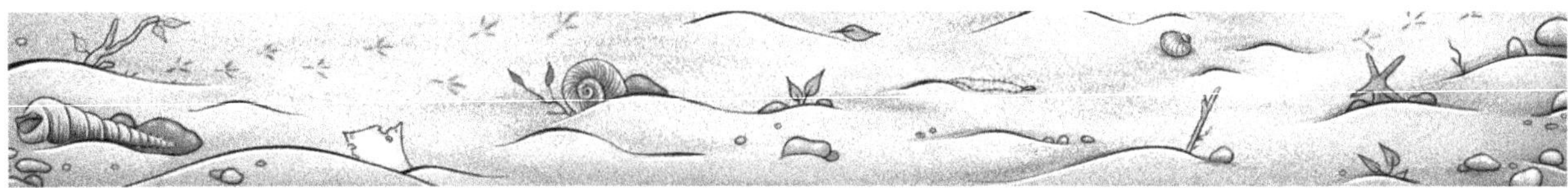

Beside Still Waters

a personal time of meditation and prayer

Read John 1 and 2 to see the events surrounding Jesus' miracle in Cana. Check out the meditation methods on page 100 to see if you would like to use one as you reflect on these Scriptures.

What do you think Jesus' disciples learned about him in these chapters?

Think of a time when God helped you get through a tough situation. Thank him for his help, and ask him to help you remember his faithfulness to you next time you face a difficulty.

Close your time of reflection by thanking the Lord for his faithfulness to answer prayer.

O magnify the Lord with me,
and let us exalt his name together.
I sought the Lord, and he answered me
and delivered me from all my fears. (Psalm 34:3–4)

~Notes~

Chapter 4: Redirected Lives on the Shores of Galilee

Reflect

Are you an impulsive person who enjoys abrupt changes and spur-of-the-moment activities, or do you prefer an orderly, scheduled life?

Gospel Focus

The Sea of Galilee (also known as Gennesaret) is the scene of many events during Jesus' life on earth. Today we are looking at a memorable event in Luke 5. Jesus is speaking to a large crowd:

> *Once while Jesus was standing beside the Lake of Gennesaret and the crowd was pressing in on him to hear the word of God, he saw two boats there at the shore of the lake; the fishermen had gotten out of them and were washing their nets. He got into one of the boats, the one belonging to Simon, and asked him to put out a little way from the shore. Then he sat down and taught the crowds from the boat. When he had finished speaking, he said to Simon, "Put out into the deep water and let down your nets for a catch."*
>
> *Simon answered, "Master, we have worked all night long but have caught nothing. Yet if you say so, I will let down the nets." (Luke 5:1-5)*

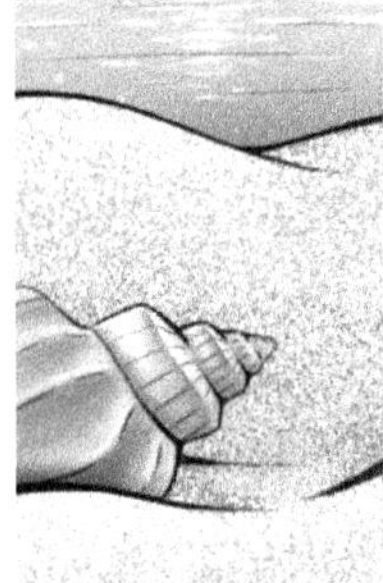

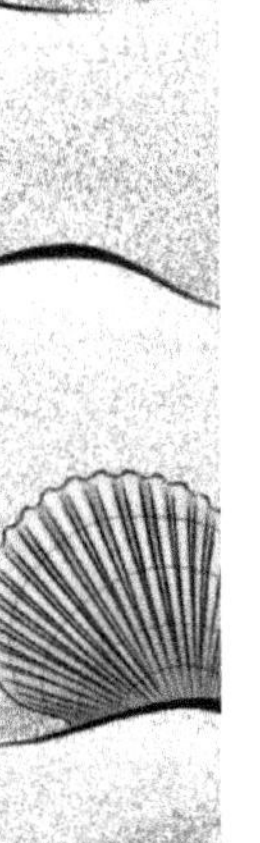

Jesus asks Simon Peter to row him out a little way from the shore so that he can more easily speak to the whole group of people. This request is an interruption to Simon's routine; he is busy cleaning his nets from a fruitless night of fishing. Perhaps he is hoping to go home soon to sleep after his long night.

This is not Simon Peter's first meeting with Jesus. Simon's brother Andrew introduced him to Jesus soon after Jesus' baptism (John 1:42). Jesus performed several miracles in Simon's hometown (Capernaum), including the healing of Simon's mother-in-law (Luke 4:48) before this boating story.

Simon Peter, an experienced fisherman, must be startled when this carpenter-turned-rabbi tells him how to fish. During daylight hours, the fish tend to hide in the deepest darkest portions of the lake, out of the reach of any fisherman's nets. Letting down the nets in broad daylight is a ridiculous idea. There is a large crowd present, and I would not be surprised if Simon is just a little worried about his reputation as a skilled fisherman if he starts fishing at this time of day.

Simon decides to trust Jesus' instruction: "If you say so, I will let down the nets." (These words express the same kind of faith as Mary's statement in John 2: "Do whatever he tells you.")

When they had done this, they caught so many fish that their nets were beginning to burst. So they signaled their partners in the other boat to come and help them. And they came and filled both boats, so that they began to sink.

But when Simon Peter saw it, he fell down at Jesus's knees, saying, "Go away from me, Lord, for I am a sinful man!" For he and all who were with him were astounded at the catch of fish that they had taken, and so also were James and John, sons of Zebedee, who were partners with Simon.

Then Jesus said to Simon, "Do not be afraid; from now on you will be catching people." When they had brought their boats to shore, they left everything and followed him. (Luke 5:6-11)

Obviously, Jesus' instructions are valid. Simon Peter has to call for reinforcements. And in the midst of the rush to haul in the huge catch of fish, Simon Peter realizes the holiness of Jesus. Only God could command a miraculous catch like this, and God is holy–completely separate from and untouched by sin. As he contrasts himself with the Holy One in his boat, Simon Peter is overcome by the knowledge of his own sinfulness.

Jesus sees Simon's heart and his growing awareness of Jesus' identity. He calla Simon and his coworkers, James and John (and probably Simon's brother Andrew also), to join him in catching or fishing for people. Several Old Testament authors had used the word picture of fishing for people in terms of judgment (Jeremiah 16:16; Ezekiel 29:4-6; Habakkuk 1:14-17, Amos 4:2) but Jesus makes this phrase an illustration of sharing the good news of the gospel.

Jesus replied to Simon, "Don't be afraid! From now on you'll be fishing for people!" (Luke 5:10 NLT)

Reflect

Considering the Scriptures we just read, how would you describe Jesus?

What do you admire about Simon Peter in the above Scriptures?

Why do you think it was life-changing for Peter to realize his sinfulness?

Overflowing Truth

Looking back at this story, I see two particularly memorable details about Simon Peter:

- Simon Peter hears this life-changing call to follow Jesus when he is in the middle of his everyday profession.
- Simon responds to Jesus with trust and obedience: "If you say so, I will."

The lesson I see in these two points is that Jesus often calls to us, interrupts us, or redirects us when we are in the middle of our daily activities. It's great to go on a retreat to spend some time focused on Jesus, but he is just as present with us in our everyday lives. Like Peter, I want to respond in obedience when I sense Jesus calling me.

As you read these Scriptures, look for truths that will encourage you the next time your life is interrupted or redirected.

I have not come to call the righteous but sinners to repentance. (Luke 5:32)
For the Son of Man came to seek out and to save the lost. *(Luke 19:10)*
But now thus says the Lord,
he who created you, O Jacob,
he who formed you, O Israel:
Do not fear, for I have redeemed you;
I have called you by name; you are mine. *(Isaiah 43:1)*
For surely I know the plans I have for you, says the Lord,
plans for your welfare and not for harm,
to give you a future with hope. (Jeremiah 29:11)
The human mind plans the way, but the Lord directs the steps. *(Proverbs 16:9)*
I will instruct you and teach you the way you should go;
I will counsel you with my eye upon you. (Psalm 32:8)
The Lord will fulfill his purpose for me;
your steadfast love, O Lord, endures forever.
Do not forsake the work of your hands. *(Psalm 138:8)*
I am confident of this, that the one who began a good work in you
will continue to complete it until the day of Jesus Christ. (Philippians 1:6)
For we are what he has made us, created in Christ Jesus for good works,
which God prepared beforehand so that we may walk in them. *(Ephesians 2:10)*

Reflect

What encouraging truths did you see in the above Scriptures?

A Redirected Life on the Nile

Our supplementary Scripture passage introduces a man whose life was redirected before he was even old enough to be aware of everything that was happening to him. In Exodus 2, the Israelites are living in slavery in Egypt. The Pharoah is concerned that this group of people is becoming too numerous, so he has ordered that all the male babies be killed at birth.

> *About this time, a man and woman from the tribe of Levi got married. The woman became pregnant and gave birth to a son. She saw that he was a special baby and kept him hidden for three months. But when she could no longer hide him, she got a basket made of papyrus reeds and waterproofed it with tar and pitch. She put the baby in the basket and laid it among the reeds along the bank of the Nile River. The baby's sister then stood at a distance, watching to see what would happen to him. (Exodus 2:1-4 NLT)*

Moses' mother manages to keep him hidden for three months, but I am guessing the baby has probably developed quite the vocal volume by this time. So she hides the baby in a floating basket among the reeds in the river. Miriam, his older sister, stands by, keeping watch.

Reflect

What dangers might have lurked in the river? What do you think Moses' mother expected to happen?

> *Soon Pharaoh's daughter came down to bathe in the river, and her attendants walked along the riverbank. When the princess saw the basket among the reeds, she sent her maid to get it for her. When the princess opened it, she saw the baby. The little boy was crying, and she felt sorry for him. "This must be one of the Hebrew children," she said.*
>
> *Then the baby's sister approached the princess. "Should I go and find one of the Hebrew women to nurse the baby for you?" she asked.*
>
> *"Yes, do!" the princess replied. So the girl went and called the baby's mother. "Take this baby and nurse him for me," the princess told the baby's mother. "I will pay you for your help." So the woman took her baby home and nursed him.*
>
> *Later, when the boy was older, his mother brought him back to Pharaoh's daughter, who adopted him as her own son. The princess named him Moses, for she explained, "I lifted him out of the water." (Exodus 2:5-10 NLT)*

This event on the shores of the Nile would have repercussions throughout Moses' life. Growing up in this wealthy household would give Moses an excellent education, preparing him for his future leadership role. But

eventually, he would have to choose whether to align himself with the family of Pharoah or his birth family.

Reflect

Put yourself in Moses' mother's position for a moment. Imagine your daughter running to you with the message that you were being given the job of wetnurse to your own son. Imagine seeing your infant son in the arms of a foreign (and pagan) princess. What thoughts would be going through your mind?

The author of Hebrews sums up Moses' story this way:

> *By faith Moses was hidden by his parents for three months after his birth, because they saw that the child was beautiful, and they were not afraid of the king's edict. By faith Moses, when he was grown up, refused to be called a son of Pharaoh's daughter, choosing rather to share ill-treatment with the people of God than to enjoy the fleeting pleasures of sin. He considered abuse suffered for the Christ to be greater wealth than the treasures of Egypt, for he was looking ahead to the reward. By faith he left Egypt, unafraid of the king's anger, for he persevered as though he saw him who is invisible. (Hebrews 11:23-27)*

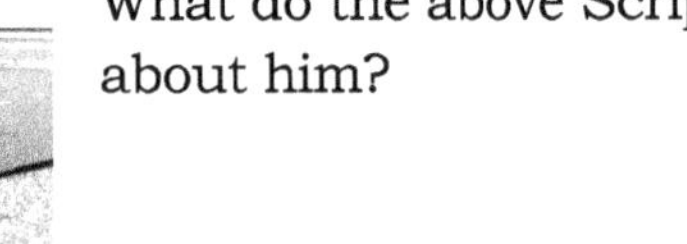

Reflect

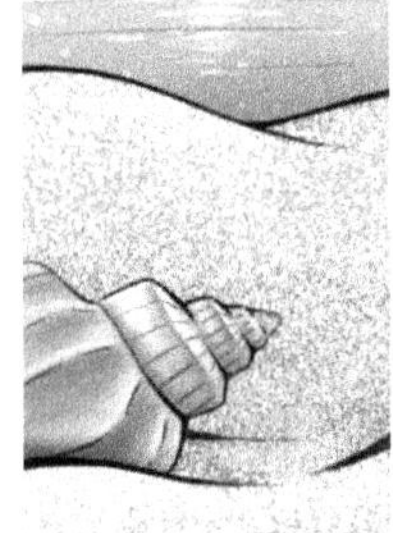

What do the above Scriptures tell you about Moses? What do you admire about him?

As you think about Peter and Moses, what do these biblical people teach us about interruptions and redirections in our own lives?

Closing Prayer

Now may the God of peace, who brought back from the dead our Lord Jesus,
the great shepherd of the sheep, by the blood of the eternal covenant,
make you complete in everything good so that you may do his will,
as he works among us that which is pleasing in his sight,
through Jesus Christ, to whom be the glory forever. Amen. (Hebrews 13:20-21)

~Notes~

Beside Still Waters

a personal time of meditation and prayer

Read Luke 5 to see the events that followed Jesus' redirection of Simon Peter's life, using one of the meditation ideas from page 100 if you desire.

Think about a time when your life was suddenly redirected. Talk to the Lord about how you feel about that experience and what you learned from it

.

What is on your agenda this week? Pray about your activities (or your lack of them), and ask the Lord's leading. Ask him to help you be sensitive to his guidance.

Do you know someone who is struggling to find direction or to begin a new chapter in their lives? Perhaps you are in this situation yourself. Talk to the Lord about this.

Close your time with the Lord by asking him to give you the courage to follow him in whatever direction he takes you.

> *Commit your way to the Lord;*
> *trust in him, and he will act. (Psalm 37:5)*

~Notes~

Chapter 5: Conversation at a Well

Reflect

Think about the location where you grew up. Was there an area of town or a neighboring town that you or your neighbors looked down upon or made jokes about? Or did you live in an area that you felt was looked down upon by others?

Gospel Focus

Here is a story of Jesus traveling through an area that his own people looked down upon:

> *[Jesus] left Judea and started back to Galilee. But he had to go through Samaria. So he came to a Samaritan city called Sychar, near the plot of ground that Jacob had given to his son Joseph. Jacob's well was there, and Jesus, tired out by his journey, was sitting by the well. It was about noon.*
>
> *A Samaritan woman came to draw water, and Jesus said to her, "Give me a drink." (His disciples had gone to the city to buy food.)*
>
> *The Samaritan woman said to him, "How is it that you, a Jew, ask a drink of me, a woman of Samaria?" (Jews do not share things in common with Samaritans.)*
> *(John 4:3-9)*

The first detail that grabs my attention here is that Jesus is "tired out by his journey." Statements that remind me of Jesus' humanity always make me pause for a moment and ponder the amazing fact that the Creator chose to live as a human on earth.

Samaritans were descended from Jewish people who intermarried with other ethnic groups. They didn't follow the Jewish religion very closely, mixing elements of other beliefs with it. At this time in Jewish history, most of the rigidly religious Jews carefully avoided traveling through Samaria. Many of them would travel a longer route to bypass it.[1] But Jesus "had to go through Samaria," perhaps for the sake of this specific encounter.

> *Jesus answered her, "If you knew the gift of God and who it is that is saying to you, 'Give me a drink,' you would have asked him, and he would have given you living water."*
>
> *The woman said to him, "Sir, you have no bucket, and the well is deep. Where do you get that living water? Are you greater than our ancestor Jacob, who gave us the well and with his sons and his flocks drank from it?"*
>
> *Jesus said to her, "Everyone who drinks of this water will be thirsty again, but those who drink of the water that I will give them will never be thirsty. The water that I will give will become in them a spring of water gushing up to eternal life."*

The woman said to him, "Sir, give me this water, so that I may never be thirsty or have to keep coming here to draw water."

Jesus said to her, "Go, call your husband, and come back."

The woman answered him, "I have no husband."

Jesus said to her, "You are right in saying, 'I have no husband,' for you have had five husbands, and the one you have now is not your husband. What you have said is true!" (John 4:10-18)

We could jump to conclusions here and presume that the woman has lost five marriages due to adultery. But in her era of low life expectancy, it was not uncommon for a woman to be widowed several times. The Scripture doesn't tell us who she is sharing a home with at this time. Widowed or unmarried women were unlikely to live alone, often living with their father, brother, or uncle. I read several ideas that she could have been in a relationship with a high-class Roman who was not allowed to marry someone of a lower class. All we really know about this woman is that she has experienced the loss of several spouses. She has not had an easy life.

The woman said to him, "Sir, I see that you are a prophet. Our ancestors worshiped on this mountain, but you say that the place where people must worship is in Jerusalem."

Jesus said to her, "Woman, believe me, the hour is coming when you will worship the Father neither on this mountain nor in Jerusalem. You worship what you do not know; we worship what we know, for salvation is from the Jews. But the hour is coming and is now here when the true worshipers will worship the Father in spirit and truth, for the Father seeks such as these to worship him. God is spirit, and those who worship him must worship in spirit and truth."

The woman said to him, "I know that Messiah is coming" (who is called Christ). "When he comes, he will proclaim all things to us."

Jesus said to her, "I am he, the one who is speaking to you." (John 4:19-26)

The conversation moves past small talk. Jesus and the woman discuss the differences in worship between the Samaritans and the Jews. When she mentions the Messiah, Jesus tells her that she is talking to him. This is astounding! Jesus tended to share his identity through actions and parables; he didn't often proclaim who he was in such obvious statements. But as he talks with this woman, he tells her plainly that he is the Messiah.

Just then his disciples came. They were astonished that he was speaking with a woman, but no one said, "What do you want?" or, "Why are you speaking with her?"

Then the woman left her water jar and went back to the city. She said to the people, "Come and see a man who told me everything I have ever done! He cannot be the Messiah, can he?" They left the city and were on their way to him. (John 4:27-30)

...Many Samaritans from that city believed in him because of the woman's testimony, "He told me everything I have ever done." So when the Samaritans came to him, they asked him to stay with them, and he stayed there two days. And many more believed because of his word... (John 4: 39-41)

The woman dashes into town to share what she has just heard. Her acquaintances invite Jesus to stay for several days, and many of them believe in him.

In the Orthodox branches of the Christian faith, the woman has a name: Photini. They consider her to be equal to the Apostles because she was an evangelist to her town. Jesus truly gave her living water, "a spring of water gushing up to eternal life."[2]

Reflect

How would you describe Jesus in this story? What kind of a person is he?

Overflowing Truth

The first overflowing truth I noticed was that God is seeking worshipers. This is my favorite aspect of this story. Just as Jesus initiated the conversation with this woman, he is still reaching out to us today, inviting us into his family of faith.

Listen! I am standing at the door, knocking; if you hear my voice and open the door,
I will come in and eat with you, and you with me. (Revelation 3:20)
The Lord looks down from heaven on humankind
to see if there are any who are wise, who seek after God. (Psalm 14:2)
For the Son of Man came to seek out and to save the lost. (Luke 19:10)
Draw near to God, and he will draw near to you...(James 4:8)

I also noticed the truth that God is a spirit. Although he cannot be contained in one place of worship, he chooses to dwell with humble repentant people.

The God who made the world and everything in it,
he who is Lord of heaven and earth,
does not live in shrines made by human hands. (Acts 17:24)
The high and lofty one who lives in eternity, the Holy One, says this:
"I live in the high and holy place
with those whose spirits are contrite and humble.
I restore the crushed spirit of the humble
and revive the courage of those with repentant hearts." (Isaiah 57:15 NLT)

Lastly, I noticed that simple conversations can lead to spiritual discussions. I was fascinated by the way Jesus took the opportunity of asking for a drink to draw this woman into a conversation. And the simple superficial conversation suddenly took a turn toward deep spiritual truths. This is a good reminder that the Lord can direct our own conversations into opportunities to gently share his truth.

...Always be ready to make your defense
to anyone who demands from you
an accounting for the hope that is in you,
yet do it with gentleness and respect... (I Peter 3:15-16)

It's news I'm most proud to proclaim,
this extraordinary Message of God's powerful plan
to rescue everyone who trusts him...
(Romans 1:16 The Message)
...As we have been approved by God
to be entrusted with the message of the gospel,
even so we speak, not to please mortals
but to please God, who tests our hearts.
(I Thessalonians 2:4)

Reflect

What would you say is the overflowing truth or the main point of the story of the Woman at the Well?

Which of the Scriptures or points we just read speaks to your heart today?

Praying at the River

Our second story features another woman whose life is impacted by the Messiah. In the book of Acts, Paul is on a missionary journey when he has a vision that directs him to a city called Philippi in Macedonia:

> *On the Sabbath day we went outside the gate by the river, where we supposed there was a place of prayer, and we sat down and spoke to the women who had gathered there. A certain woman named Lydia, a worshiper of God, was listening to us; she was from the city of Thyatira and a dealer in purple cloth. The Lord opened her heart to listen eagerly to what was said by Paul. When she and her household were baptized, she urged us, saying, "If you have judged me to be faithful to the Lord, come and stay at my home." And she prevailed upon us. (Acts 16:13-15)*

Because Philippi was a major city, Paul may have expected to find a Jewish synagogue there where he could share the gospel. Instead, he finds a gathering of women who met for prayer by the river.

Although not Jewish by birth, Lydia worshiped the God of the Jews. She was a dealer in purple cloth, an expensive material that was available only to the wealthy, who wore it and covered their couches with it. Lydia seems to be an independent woman. (The text mentions "her household," and she refers to "my home.") Paul and his companions (Silas, and probably Timothy and Luke) accept Lydia's offer of hospitality. If you read the remaining verses of Acts 16, you will see that Paul and Silas were persecuted and jailed during their time in Philippi. Lydia welcomes these men into her home again after they are released from prison.[3] Lydia continued to open her home, and it became the first location of the brand new church in Philippi. (Acts 16:40).

Reflect

Looking at the few details we have about Lydia, how would you describe her?

Although Paul soon moved on to a new area, he stayed in contact with the Philippian church. The joyful book of Philippians in the New Testament is a letter he wrote to them.

> *Paul and Timothy, servants of Christ Jesus,*
> *To all the saints in Christ Jesus who are in Philippi, with the bishops and deacons:*
> *Grace to you and peace from God our Father and the Lord Jesus Christ.*
> *I thank my God for every remembrance of you, always in every one of my prayers for all of you, praying with joy for your partnership in the gospel from the first day until now.*
> *(Philippians 1:1-5)*

Just as the Samaritan woman was entrusted with a message about the Messiah, Lydia was entrusted with a partnership in the gospel. What has God entrusted to us?

> *All this is from God, who reconciled us to himself through Christ and has given us the ministry of reconciliation; that is, in Christ God was reconciling the world to himself, not counting their trespasses against them, and entrusting the message of reconciliation to us. So we are ambassadors for Christ...*
> *(2 Corinthians 5:18-20)*

Reflect

What do you see as the challenges of being an ambassador for Christ in our society today?

Closing Prayer

Let the words of my mouth and the meditation of my heart be acceptable to you, O Lord, my rock and my redeemer. (Psalm 19:14)

~Notes~

Beside Still Waters

a personal time of meditation and prayer

Look back at 2 Corinthians 5:18-20. What does it mean to you when you read that you are an ambassador for Christ? What does that look like in practical terms?

Here are a few verses from Philippians 1. Notice Paul's attitude towards the believers and what he is praying for them:

> *I am confident of this, that the one who began a good work in you*
> *will continue to complete it until the day of Jesus Christ.*
> *It is right for me to think this way about all of you,*
> *because I hold you in my heart,*
> *for all of you are my partners in God's grace,*
> *both in my imprisonment and in the defense and confirmation of the gospel.*
> *For God is my witness, how I long for all of you with the tender affection of Christ Jesus.*
> *And this is my prayer, that your love may overflow more and more with knowledge*
> *and full insight to help you to determine what really matters,*
> *so that in the day of Christ you may be pure and blameless,*
> *having produced the harvest of righteousness that comes through Jesus Christ*
> *for the glory and praise of God. (Philippians 1:6-11)*

Read the above passage again, and look for

- a phrase or two that you can use as you praise God
- a phrase or two that you can use in your prayers for yourself
- a phrase or two that you can use as you pray for others.
- Read about Colorful Meditation in the Appendix. Consider using these phrases in this meditation method.

Close your time of prayer by thanking the Lord that his word is available to you, and praying for those who have not yet heard his Good News.

~Notes~

Chapter 6: Enlightenment Near a Pool

Reflect

What benefits does light (sunlight as well as indoor light) bring to our daily lives?

Gospel Focus

Today's story shows us a man who has lived with blindness for many years. When a meeting with Jesus changes his life, the truth about Jesus gradually dawns upon him.

> *As he [Jesus] walked along, he saw a man blind from birth. His disciples asked him, "Rabbi, who sinned, this man or his parents, that he was born blind?"*
>
> *Jesus answered, "Neither this man nor his parents sinned; he was born blind so that God's works might be revealed in him.* (John 9:1-3)

The story begins with an essential truth: suffering is not always caused by sin. This is a truth to cling to when we experience tough times or we interact with others who are in the midst of trials. Here in John 9, this man's condition would reveal the work of God and the identity of Jesus.

> *We must work the works of him who sent me while it is day; night is coming, when no one can work. As long as I am in the world, I am the light of the world." When he had said this, he spat on the ground and made mud with the saliva and spread the mud on the man's eyes, saying to him, "Go, wash in the pool of Siloam" (which means Sent). Then he went and washed and came back able to see.* (John 9:4-7)

After proclaiming that he is the light of the world, Jesus begins to bring light to a man who has lived in a dark world his whole life. Although it sounds odd to us, healers in the ancient world sometimes used their own spit as an ingredient in their treatments.[1] Jesus uses spittle and dirt to make a clay poultice, places it on the man's eyes, and sends him to the pool of Siloam to wash. You might remember the pool of Siloam from our reading in chapter one: it was the source of the sacred water used at the Feast of Tabernacles.

Reflect

Why do you think the man followed Jesus' instructions? What was there about Jesus' voice or words that inspired such confidence, even from this man who could not see him?

The neighbors and those who had seen him before as a beggar began to ask, "Is this not the man who used to sit and beg?" Some were saying, "It is he." Others were saying, "No, but it is someone like him."

He kept saying, "I am he."

But they kept asking him, "Then how were your eyes opened?"

He answered, "The man called Jesus made mud, spread it on my eyes, and said to me, 'Go to Siloam and wash.' Then I went and washed and received my sight."

They said to him, "Where is he?"

He said, "I do not know." (John 9:8-12)

The now-healed man has only a few moments to enjoy his new sight before he is badgered with questions about how this happened. At this point, he refers to "the man called Jesus" as the source of his healing. The questions turn into an interrogation. The Pharisees are not investigating the healing to find out more about an amazing miracle but to blame Jesus for working on the Sabbath.

They brought to the Pharisees the man who had formerly been blind. Now it was a Sabbath day when Jesus made the mud and opened his eyes. Then the Pharisees also began to ask him how he had received his sight.

He said to them, "He put mud on my eyes. Then I washed, and now I see."

Some of the Pharisees said, "This man is not from God, for he does not observe the Sabbath." Others said, "How can a man who is a sinner perform such signs?" And they were divided. So they said again to the blind man, "What do you say about him? It was your eyes he opened."

He said, "He is a prophet." (John 9:13-17)

Here we have the formerly blind man declaring that Jesus is a prophet. His ideas about Jesus are developing rapidly.

The Jews did not believe that he had been blind and had received his sight until they called the parents of the man who had received his sight and asked them, "Is this your son, who you say was born blind? How then does he now see?"

His parents answered, "We know that this is our son and that he was born blind, but we do not know how it is that now he sees, nor do we know who opened his eyes. Ask him; he is of age. He will speak for himself." His parents said this because they were afraid of the Jews, for the Jews had already agreed that anyone who confessed Jesus to be the Messiah would be put out of the synagogue. Therefore his parents said, "He is of age; ask him." (John 9:18-23)

In these Scriptures, when you see the phrase "the Jews," it refers to those Pharisees who were more focused on the tiniest details of their law than on the needs of people. More concerned with power than with faith, these leaders had decided to excommunicate anyone who declared that Jesus was the Messiah. This exclusion was more than just prohibiting people from weekly worship services. The synagogue was the center of Jewish cultural identity, and those who were "put out" could be shunned by friends and relatives in their daily activities.

So for the second time they called the man who had been blind, and they said to him, "Give glory to God! We know that this man is a sinner."

He answered, "I do not know whether he is a sinner. One thing I do know, that though I was blind, now I see."

They said to him, "What did he do to you? How did he open your eyes?"

He answered them, "I have told you already, and you would not listen. Why do you want to hear it again? Do you also want to become his disciples?"

Then they reviled him, saying, "You are his disciple, but we are disciples of Moses. We know that God has spoken to Moses, but as for this man, we do not know where he comes from."

The man answered, "Here is an astonishing thing! You do not know where he comes from, yet he opened my eyes. We know that God does not listen to sinners, but he does listen to one who worships him and obeys his will. Never since the world began has it been heard that anyone opened the eyes of a person born blind. If this man were not from God, he could do nothing."

They answered him, "You were born entirely in sins, and are you trying to teach us?" And they drove him out. (John 9:24-34)

In the midst of this tense situation, the healed man displays a sense of humor as he asks the Pharisees if they also want to become disciples of Jesus. Then he shares an astonishing truth: he has come to realize that Jesus has come from God.

By this time the Pharisees are enraged. They tell the man he is sinful, and they cast him out of the synagogue.

Reflect

He bagan the day blind, but was healed, interrogated, and banned from the synagogue by evening. What do you think he is thinking and feeling?

Jesus heard that they had driven him out, and when he found him he said, "Do you believe in the Son of Man?"

He answered, "And who is he, sir? Tell me, so that I may believe in him."

Jesus said to him, "You have seen him, and the one speaking with you is he."

He said, "Lord, I believe." And he worshiped him. (John 9:35-38)

Jesus hears all that has happened to the man, and he seeks him out. Jesus tells him that he is the Son of Man. (This phrase is used in the book of Daniel to describe a heavenly being who has everlasting dominion over the earth. It is one of the titles of the Messiah.)

The story ends with the man worshipping the Messiah who gave him his sight.

Overflowing Truth

The Bible uses the concepts of darkness and light to describe our spiritual journeys. As you read the next set of Scriptures, notice how the light of the Lord changes our lives.

...I am the light of the world. Whoever follows me
will never walk in darkness but will have the light of life. (John 8:12)
May you be made strong with all the strength
that comes from his glorious power,
so that you may have all endurance and patience,
joyfully giving thanks to the Father,
who has enabled you to share in the inheritance of the saints in the light.
He has rescued us from the power of darkness and transferred us
into the kingdom of his beloved Son, in whom we have redemption,
***the forgiveness of sins.** (Colossians 1:11-14)*
For once you were full of darkness, but now you have light from the Lord.
So live as people of light! For this light within you
produces only what is good and right and true.
***Carefully determine what pleases the Lord.** (Ephesians 5:8-10 NLT)*

Reflect

What did the above verses tell you about lives changing from darkness to light?

We began this chapter thinking of the benefits of light in the natural world and inside our homes. What similarities do those benefits have with spiritual enlightenment from God?

A Contrast at the Pool of Beth-zatha

Our second story today tells of another healing near a pool. Ancient people, both Jews and pagans, believed that the Pool of Beth-zatha (also called Bethesda or Bethsaida) had healing properties.[2]

...There was a festival of the Jews, and Jesus went up to Jerusalem. Now in Jerusalem by the Sheep Gate there is a pool, called in Hebrew Beth-zatha, which has five porticoes. In these lay many ill, blind, lame, and paralyzed people. One man was there who had been ill for thirty-eight years. When Jesus saw him lying there and knew that he had been there a long time, he said to him, "Do you want to be made well?" (John 5:1-6)

Reflect

Use your imagination to think of a few reasons why the man might not want to be healed.

The ill man answered him, "Sir, I have no one to put me into the pool when the water is stirred up, and while I am making my way someone else steps down ahead of me."

Jesus said to him, "Stand up, take your mat and walk." At once the man was made well, and he took up his mat and began to walk.

Now that day was a Sabbath. So the Jews said to the man who had been cured, "It is the Sabbath; it is not lawful for you to carry your mat."

But he answered them, "The man who made me well said to me, 'Take up your mat and walk.' "

They asked him, "Who is the man who said to you, 'Take it up and walk'?" Now the man who had been healed did not know who it was, for Jesus had disappeared in the crowd that was there.

Later Jesus found him in the temple and said to him, "See, you have been made well! Do not sin any more, so that nothing worse happens to you."

The man went away and told the Jews that it was Jesus who had made him well. Therefore the Jews started persecuting Jesus, because he was doing such things on the Sabbath. (John 5:7–16)

Like the blind man, the formerly crippled man finds himself being questioned about his healing. And just as he did for the blind man, Jesus sought him out. He found him in the temple and urged him not to sin anymore so that nothing worse will happen to him. (This leads me to wonder if this man's condition had somehow been the result of his own choices.) The healed man tells the Jewish leaders that his healer is Jesus, and as a result, the leaders begin persecuting Jesus. There is no journey of faith recorded for this man.

Reflect

What differences do you see between the two men?

How does God's word bring enlightenment to our lives?

Closing Prayer

Your word is a lamp to my feet
and a light to my path. (Psalm 119:105)
You light a lamp for me.
The Lord, my God, lights up my darkness. (Psalm 18:28)

~Notes~

Beside Still Waters

a personal time of meditation and prayer

Take some time to meditate on John 9 or on the Overflowing Truth verses. You may want to use one of the meditation ideas on page 100 or 101.

> *One thing I do know, that though I was blind, now I see. (John 9:25)*

As you look at the above statement, consider what your one-sentence testimony might be. Don't try to sum up your whole life story. Just think of a way in which the Lord has changed or made a difference in your life. You may want to limit this to the last five or ten years.

Close your time in prayer by thanking the Lord for being with you even in the dark seasons of life.

> *For you have delivered my soul from death*
> *and my feet from falling,*
> *so that I may walk before God*
> *in the light of life. (Psalm 56:13)*

~Notes~

Chapter 7: Panic on the Sea of Galilee

Reflect

How do you feel about boat journeys? Are they a great idea for a vacation? Or do you feel a little panic at the thought of not having firm ground under your feet?

Gospel Focus

In today's story, Jesus has just finished a long day of teaching on the shores of Lake Galilee.

> *On that day, when evening had come, he said to them, "Let us go across to the other side." And leaving the crowd behind, they took him with them in the boat, just as he was. Other boats were with him. A great windstorm arose, and the waves beat into the boat, so that the boat was already being swamped. (Mark 4:35–37)*

The Sea of Galilee is below sea level, and it is surrounded by hills that can funnel sudden stormy winds into the sea. Many of the disciples are fishermen by trade, so they are accustomed to storms at sea. They are vividly aware of the storm's power and the possibility of shipwreck.

> *But he was in the stern, asleep on the cushion, and they woke him up and said to him, "Teacher, do you not care that we are perishing?" (Mark 4:38)*

This verse gives us another touching portrait of Jesus' humanity. The Son of God has come to earth in a human body that has become exhausted and even appreciates a bit of a cushion while he is napping.

The disciples see their Master sleeping through one of the the biggest storms they've ever encountered, and they are astounded. Does Jesus care about them? Surely he should be helping them survive! They cry out to him in panic.

> *And waking up, he rebuked the wind and said to the sea, "Be silent! Be still!" Then the wind ceased, and there was a dead calm. He said to them, "Why are you afraid? Have you still no faith?"*
>
> *And they were filled with great fear and said to one another, "Who then is this, that even the wind and the sea obey him?" (Mark 5:39–41)*

Jesus' power over the natural world is visible as he rebukes the wind and silences the sea.

Reflect

Why do you think the disciples were so fearful when they saw Jesus' great power?

The powerful Son of God has come to this group of men, has been listening to their doubts and their petty squabbles, and heard their anguished cry: "Don't you care about us?"

We know the answer. We know that, of course, Jesus cared about them. But we understand their question. We have all experienced storms that caused us to cry out to God in panic.

Overflowing Truth

It is truly a life-changing moment when we realize that the mighty powerful Creator cares for each of us. It is a truth we can discover over and over.

O Lord, what are human beings that you should notice them,
mere mortals that you should think about them?
For they are like a breath of air;
their days are like a passing shadow.
Open the heavens, Lord, and come down.
Touch the mountains so they billow smoke.
Hurl your lightning bolts and scatter your enemies!
Shoot your arrows and confuse them!
Reach down from heaven and rescue me;
rescue me from deep waters,
from the power of my enemies. (Psalm 144:3-7 NLT)

Reflect

In the verses above from Psalm 144, how would you describe the author's attitude? What is he pondering, and what is he depending on God to do?

In the following segment of Psalm 107, we see a poetic description of an experience that is very similar to the disciples in the storm.

Some went down to the sea in ships,
doing business on the mighty waters;
they saw the deeds of the Lord,
his wondrous works in the deep.
For he commanded and raised the stormy wind,
which lifted up the waves of the sea.
They mounted up to heaven; they went down to the depths;
their courage melted away in their calamity;

they reeled and staggered like drunkards
and were at their wits' end.
Then they cried to the Lord in their trouble,
and he brought them out from their distress;
he made the storm be still,
and the waves of the sea were hushed.
Then they were glad because they had quiet,
and he brought them to their desired haven.
Let them thank the Lord for his steadfast love,
for his wonderful works to humankind. (Psalm 107:23-31)

Reflect

What happened to the people in Psalm 107 when they cried to the Lord?

A Dry Path through the Sea

The story we just read in Mark 4 brought to my mind an Old Testament event. I wonder if the disciples thought of this incident as they struggled to understand who Jesus was.

In Exodus 14, the Israelites have just escaped their lives of slavery in Egypt, and they are headed for the promised land at last. But Pharoah, realizing what he has lost in terms of his labor force, pursues them. The Israelites, with Pharoah's army creeping up on them and the Red Sea in front of them, are understandably in a bit of a panic.

As Pharaoh drew near, the Israelites looked back, and there were the Egyptians advancing on them. In great fear the Israelites cried out to the Lord. They said to Moses, "Was it because there were no graves in Egypt that you have taken us away to die in the wilderness? What have you done to us, bringing us out of Egypt? Is this not the very thing we told you in Egypt, 'Let us alone so that we can serve the Egyptians'? For it would have been better for us to serve the Egyptians than to die in the wilderness."

But Moses said to the people, "Do not be afraid, stand firm, and see the deliverance that the Lord will accomplish for you today, for the Egyptians whom you see today you shall never see again. The Lord will fight for you, and you have only to keep still."

Then the Lord said to Moses, "Why do you cry out to me? Tell the Israelites to go forward. But you lift up your staff and stretch out your hand over the sea and divide it, that the Israelites may go into the sea on dry ground..."

Then Moses stretched out his hand over the sea. The Lord drove the sea back by a strong east wind all night and turned the sea into dry land, and the waters were divided. The Israelites went into the sea on dry ground, the waters forming a wall for them on their right and on their left.

The Egyptians pursued and went into the sea after them, all of Pharaoh's horses, chariots, and chariot drivers. At the morning watch the Lord, in the pillar of fire and cloud, looked down on the Egyptian army and threw the Egyptian army into a panic. He clogged their chariot wheels so that they turned with difficulty. The Egyptians said, "Let us flee

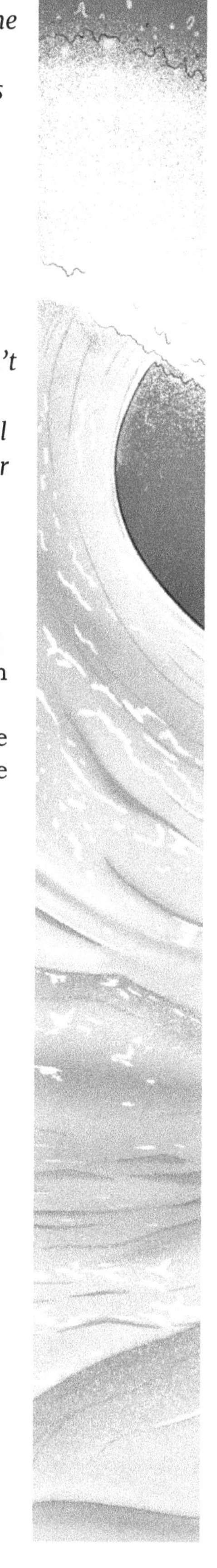

from the Israelites, for the Lord is fighting for them against Egypt."

Then the Lord said to Moses, "Stretch out your hand over the sea, so that the water may come back upon the Egyptians, upon their chariots and chariot drivers."...But the Israelites walked on dry ground through the sea, the waters forming a wall for them on their right and on their left. (Exodus 14:10-29)

I appreciated the dramatic phrases used in the people's words in the New Living Translation:

As Pharaoh approached, the people of Israel looked up and panicked when they saw the Egyptians overtaking them. They cried out to the Lord, and they said to Moses, "Why did you bring us out here to die in the wilderness? Weren't there enough graves for us in Egypt? What have you done to us? Why did you make us leave Egypt? Didn't we tell you this would happen while we were still in Egypt? We said, 'Leave us alone! Let us be slaves to the Egyptians. It's better to be a slave in Egypt than a corpse in the wilderness!'"

But Moses told the people, "Don't be afraid. Just stand still and watch the Lord rescue you today..." (Exodus 14:10-13 NLT)

Just as the disciples, fearing for their lives, called out to Jesus, asking if he cared about them, so the Israelites dramatically inquired if they had been brought to the wilderness to die because there were no graves in Egypt.

These unedited cries for help remind me of the prayers of lament in the book of Psalms. Here are a few verses from two laments. Ask yourself what the tone of these prayers is and what emotions the authors are expressing.

To you, O Lord, I cried,
and to the Lord I made supplication:
"What profit is there in my death if I go down to the Pit?
Will the dust praise you?
Will it tell of your faithfulness?
Hear, O Lord, and be gracious to me!
O Lord, be my helper!" (Psalm 30:8-10)
Have compassion on me, Lord, for I am weak.
Heal me, Lord, for my bones are in agony.
I am sick at heart.
How long, O Lord, until you restore me?
Return, O Lord, and rescue me.
Save me because of your unfailing love...
I am worn out from sobbing.
All night I flood my bed with weeping,
drenching it with my tears.
My vision is blurred by grief;
my eyes are worn out because of all my enemies.
(Psalm 6:2-4, 6-7 NLT)

Reflect

How would you describe the tone of the Psalms we just read?

What kind of prayer do you find easiest to express to God?

- passionate lamenting
- a simple sharing of your heart
- thanksgiving
- agreeing in your own heart as you read or hear prayers

What kind of prayer would you add to the list?

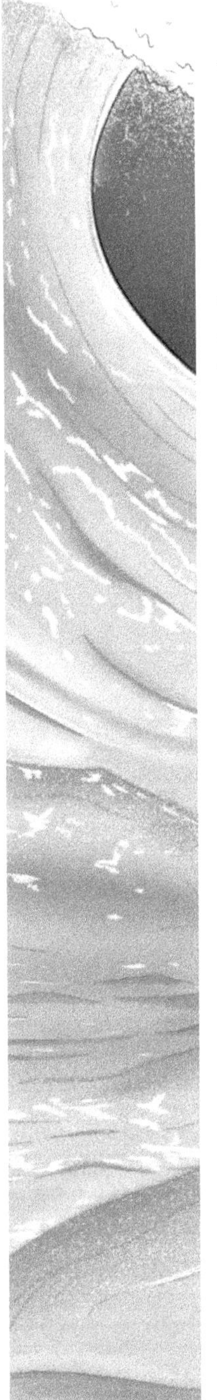

Like the disciples in their storm-tossed boat, and the Israelites on the edge of the Red Sea, we all go through times when we wonder if God really cares for us. And although God always works on his own timetable, we can be certain that he is ever present with us, hearing our prayers, and caring for us with his steadfast love.

...Do not fear, for I have redeemed you;
I have called you by name; you are mine.
When you pass through the waters,
I will be with you,
and through the rivers, they shall not overwhelm you. *(Isaiah 43:1-2)*
For who in the skies can be compared to the Lord?
Who among the heavenly beings is like the Lord,
a God feared in the council of the holy ones,
great and awesome above all who are around him?
O Lord God of hosts,
who is as mighty as you, O Lord?
Your faithfulness surrounds you. (Psalm 89:6-8)

Closing Prayer

Father in heaven, you say I won't be overwhelmed by rivers of trouble,
but I feel ready to sink today.
I cannot see you walking beside me.
I cannot feel your hand holding mine.
Remind me, Lord
of your power
your presence
and your faithfulness.

~Notes~

Beside Still Waters

a personal time of meditation and prayer

Take a few moments to meditate on Psalm 13. (This could be a good time to use the method of Colorful Meditation or Comparing Translations on page 100 or 101.) Notice how the author begins his lament by pouring out his heart to the Lord, and how he ends it by stating his conviction that he will eventually sing and rejoice over the Lord's deliverance.

How long, O Lord? Will you forget me forever?
How long will you hide your face from me?
How long must I bear pain in my soul
and have sorrow in my heart all day long?
How long shall my enemy be exalted over me?
Consider and answer me, O Lord my God!
Give light to my eyes, or I will sleep the sleep of death,
and my enemy will say, "I have prevailed";
my foes will rejoice because I am shaken.
But I trusted in your steadfast love;
my heart shall rejoice in your salvation.
I will sing to the Lord
because he has dealt bountifully with me. (Psalm 13)

Is there anything you want to lament about today? Talk with the Lord about the needs and concerns of your heart.

You may want to read Mark 4 to read the events surrounding the story we focused on today.

With my voice I cry to the Lord;
with my voice I make supplication to the Lord.
I pour out my complaint before him;
I tell my trouble before him.
When my spirit is faint,
you know my way. (Psalm 142:1-3)

~Notes~

Chapter 8: Set Free at the Seaside

Reflect

What comes to mind when you think about the word “freedom”? From what might people in your neighborhood need to be set free?

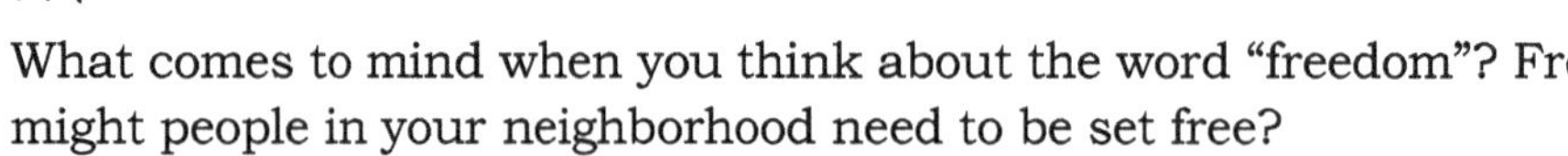

Gospel Focus

Today’s Gospel Scripture comes from Mark 5, immediately after the story of Jesus calming the storm that we read in the preceding chapter. According to Mark 5:20, this event takes place in the area of the Decapolis. This was a group of cities with a Greek background and a mixed population of Jews and other ethnic groups.

> *They came to the other side of the sea, to the region of the Gerasenes. And when he had stepped out of the boat, immediately a man from the tombs with an unclean spirit met him. He lived among the tombs, and no one could restrain him any more, even with a chain, for he had often been restrained with shackles and chains, but the chains he wrenched apart, and the shackles he broke in pieces, and no one had the strength to subdue him. Night and day among the tombs and on the mountains he was always howling and bruising himself with stones. (Mark 5:1–5)*

The topic of unclean spirits and demon possession is a large one with many different viewpoints. Let’s just focus on the fact that here is a man who is under the influence of a power from which he cannot escape. He lives a tormented life while his neighbors have literally tried to keep him in chains. As Jesus steps ashore, the troubled man meets him.

> *When he saw Jesus from a distance, he ran and bowed down before him, and he shouted at the top of his voice, “What have you to do with me, Jesus, Son of the Most High God? I adjure you by God, do not torment me.”*
>
> *For he had said to him, “Come out of the man, you unclean spirit!” Then Jesus asked him, “What is your name?”*
>
> *He replied, “My name is Legion, for we are many.” He begged him earnestly not to send them out of the region. Now there on the hillside a great herd of swine was feeding, and the unclean spirits begged him, “Send us into the swine; let us enter them.” So he gave them permission. And the unclean spirits came out and entered the swine, and the herd, numbering about two thousand, stampeded down the steep bank into the sea and were drowned in the sea. (Mark 5:6–13)*

I have to admit that my first reaction when I hear this story is always to wonder about the pigs. Why did Jesus allow them to be destroyed? What about the cost to their owners? I think this is a very human reaction. We are so easily distracted from caring about people by our worries about our belongings and our finances.

This story shows us how much Jesus values troubled people. The man's health and sanity were far more important than someone's future income from slaughtering the pigs. Don't forget that Jewish people considered pigs to be unclean. The disciples may have thought it was very appropriate that evil powers would take up residence in pigs. I think Jesus allowed this incident in order to make the miracle of healing visible. It was very obvious to everyone watching that the power that had kept the man prisoner was no longer within him.

> *The swineherds ran off and told it in the city and in the country. Then people came to see what it was that had happened. They came to Jesus and saw the man possessed by demons sitting there, clothed and in his right mind, the very man who had had the legion, and they became frightened. Those who had seen what had happened to the man possessed by demons and to the swine reported it. Then they began to beg Jesus to leave their neighborhood. (Mark 5:1-17)*

Reflect

Why do you think the people wanted Jesus to leave?

How do you think the disciples felt as they watched this situation unfold? Don't forget that they have just come through an extremely frightening storm.

> *As he was getting into the boat, the man who had been possessed by demons begged him that he might be with him. But Jesus refused and said to him, "Go home to your own people, and tell them how much the Lord has done for you and what mercy he has shown you." And he went away and began to proclaim in the Decapolis how much Jesus had done for him, and everyone was amazed. (Mark 5:18-20)*

It seems surprising to me that Jesus did not ask this man to join the group of disciples. Instead, Jesus gave him the privilege of being one of the earliest missionaries. He must have made an impact on his neighbors because the next time Jesus went ashore in the area of the Decapolis, he was a welcome guest. (Mark 7:31-32)

Overflowing Truth

This story overflows with deliverance and freedom and the power of Jesus to restore lives.

> *Then Jesus said to the Jews who had believed in him,*
> *"If you continue in my word,*

you are truly my disciples, and you will know the truth,
and the truth will make you free." (John 8:31-32)
Grace to you and peace from God our Father and the Lord Jesus Christ,
who gave himself for our sins to set us free from the present evil age,
according to the will of our God and Father,
to whom be the glory forever and ever. Amen. (Galatians 1:3-5)
Christ has set us free to live a free life.
So take your stand!
Never again let anyone put a harness of slavery on you.
(Galatians 5:1 Message)
For you were called to freedom, brothers and sisters,
only do not use your freedom as an opportunity for self-indulgence,
but through love become enslaved to one another. (Galatians 5:13)

Reflect

What did the verses above tell you about the freedom that Jesus can bring?

What instructions did the above verses give us?

Look back at your answers to the first question in this chapter. How might Jesus bring freedom in the situations you mentioned?

Freedom & Healing

For our supplementary story today, we are continuing in Mark 5. We read of a great crowd by the sea, a father who is desperate to find healing for his daughter and an interruption. It is this interruption that shows us another life set free at the seaside.

When Jesus had crossed again in the boat to the other side, a great crowd gathered around him, and he was by the sea. Then one of the leaders of the synagogue, named Jairus, came and, when he saw him, fell at his feet and pleaded with him repeatedly, "My little daughter is at the point of death. Come and lay your hands on her, so that she may be made well and live." So he went with him.

And a large crowd followed him and pressed in on him. Now there was a woman who had been suffering from a flow of blood for twelve years. She had endured much under many physicians and had spent all that she had, and she was no better but rather grew worse. She had heard about Jesus and came up behind him in the crowd and touched his cloak, for she said, "If I but touch his cloak, I will be made well."

Immediately her flow of blood stopped, and she felt in her body that she was healed of

her disease. Immediately aware that power had gone forth from him, Jesus turned about in the crowd and said, "Who touched my cloak?"

And his disciples said to him, "You see the crowd pressing in on you; how can you say, 'Who touched me?' "

He looked all around to see who had done it. But the woman, knowing what had happened to her, came in fear and trembling, fell down before him, and told him the whole truth. He said to her, "Daughter, your faith has made you well; go in peace, and be healed of your disease." (Mark 5:21-35)

You can finish Mark 5 on your own to get the rest of the story about the daughter of the synagogue leader. For now, we are focusing on the woman who is healed. She has been ill for many years. She has spent all her money on treatments that gave her no results. Her bleeding disorder makes her "unclean" under Jewish law. No one can touch her or hug her. In fact, in the normal way of things, when she reaches out to touch Jesus, she would make him "unclean." But Jesus has a way of turning things around, and in this situation, his power set her free.

Jesus could have kept this miracle private, but he asked questions that made the woman share her story.

Reflect

Why do you think Jesus wanted the woman to talk about her healing?

From this brief glimpse of the woman, how would you describe her?

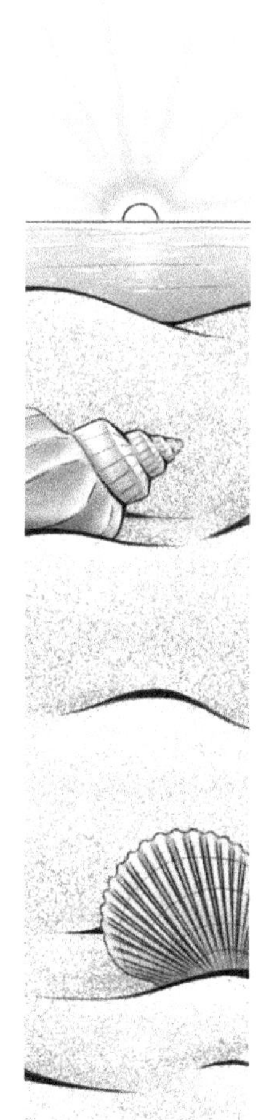

I like to picture the healed woman on her way home. I imagine her singing joyful songs. These verses from Psalms show us poetic expressions of thanksgiving for God's deliverance.

Therefore let all who are faithful
offer prayer to you;
at a time of distress,
the rush of mighty waters shall not reach them.
You are a hiding place for me;
you preserve me from trouble;
you surround me with glad cries of deliverance. Selah
(Psalm 32:6-7)
I have told the glad news of deliverance
in the great congregation;
see, I have not restrained my lips,
as you know, O Lord.

I have not hidden your saving help within my heart;
I have spoken of your faithfulness and your salvation;
I have not concealed your steadfast love and your faithfulness
from the great congregation. (Psalm 40:9–10)

Of course we all know of situations (or may have experienced them ourselves) when, for reasons we cannot understand, the Lord does not provide freedom or deliverance. There are no easy answers for these situations. Even the Apostle Paul wrote about his "thorn in the flesh," an ailment or situation from which he longed to be set free:

Three different times I begged the Lord to take it away.
Each time he said, "My grace is all you need.
My power works best in weakness."
So now I am glad to boast about my weaknesses,
so that the power of Christ can work through me.
(2 Corinthians 12:8–9 NLT)

Closing Prayer

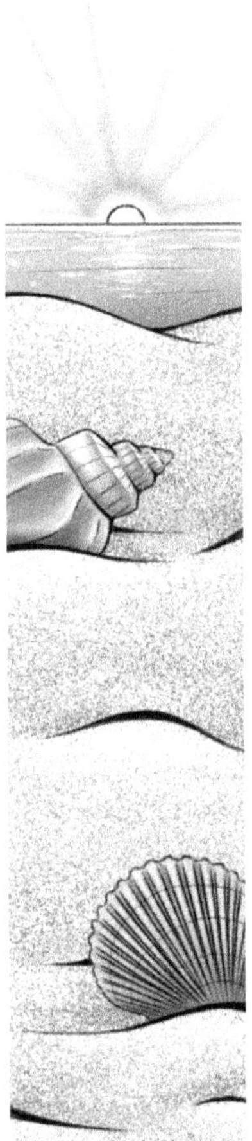

Happy are those whose help is the God of Jacob,
whose hope is in the Lord their God,
who made heaven and earth,
the sea, and all that is in them;
who keeps faith forever;
who executes justice for the oppressed;
who gives food to the hungry.
The Lord sets the prisoners free;
the Lord opens the eyes of the blind.
The Lord lifts up those who are bowed down;
the Lord loves the righteous.
The Lord watches over the strangers;
he upholds the orphan and the widow.
but the way of the wicked he brings to ruin.
The Lord will reign forever,
your God, O Zion, for all generations.
Praise the Lord! (Psalm 146:5–10)

~Notes~

Beside Still Waters

a personal time of prayer and meditation on the Scriptures

Read all of Mark 5 to get the whole story of the man who is delivered, the woman who is healed, and the sick little girl whose father begged Jesus to heal her. Suggestion: choose your favorite portion of Mark 5 and use it with the Listen & Respond meditation method on page 100.

This Psalm expresses the joy of freedom and deliverance. Perhaps you will find a few phrases you can use in a prayer.

I will exalt you, Lord, for you rescued me.
You refused to let my enemies triumph over me.
O Lord my God, I cried to you for help,
and you restored my health.
You brought me up from the grave, O Lord.
You kept me from falling into the pit of death.
Sing to the Lord, all you godly ones!
Praise his holy name.
For his anger lasts only a moment,
but his favor lasts a lifetime!
Weeping may last through the night,
but joy comes with the morning.
When I was prosperous, I said,
"Nothing can stop me now!"
Your favor, O Lord, made me as secure as a mountain.
Then you turned away from me, and I was shattered.
I cried out to you, O Lord.
I begged the Lord for mercy, saying,
"What will you gain if I die,
if I sink into the grave?
Can my dust praise you?
Can it tell of your faithfulness?
Hear me, Lord, and have mercy on me.
Help me, O Lord."
You have turned my mourning into joyful dancing.
You have taken away my clothes of mourning and clothed me with joy,
that I might sing praises to you and not be silent.
O Lord my God, I will give you thanks forever! (Psalm 30 NLT)

~Notes~

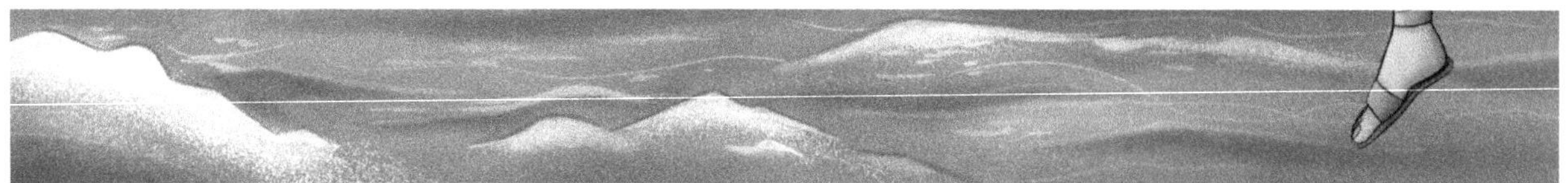

Chapter 9: Walking on the Waves

Reflect

When you were a kid, were you always the first in line to try anything new and challenging and possibly scary? Or were you the sensible kid, waiting to see how it all worked out for the other kids?

Gospel Focus

As Jesus' ministry grew, he continued to attract large crowds while he was teaching and healing. But in Matthew 14, after confronting a less-than-welcoming attitude in his hometown and receiving the news of his relative's execution (John the Baptist), Jesus is seeking some solitude on a hillside near the Sea of Galilee:

> *Immediately he made the disciples get into a boat and go on ahead to the other side, while he dismissed the crowds. And after he had dismissed the crowds, he went up the mountain by himself to pray. When evening came, he was there alone, but by this time the boat, battered by the waves, was far from the land, for the wind was against them. And early in the morning he came walking toward them on the sea.*
>
> *But when the disciples saw him walking on the sea, they were terrified, saying, "It is a ghost!" And they cried out in fear.*
>
> *But immediately Jesus spoke to them and said, "Take heart, it is I; do not be afraid." (Matthew 14:22-27)*

Some scholars believe that the phrase "it is I," was actually Jesus saying, "I Am," the ancient name of God that is used in the Old Testament.[1]

> *Peter answered him, "Lord, if it is you, command me to come to you on the water."*
>
> *He said, "Come." So Peter got out of the boat, started walking on the water, and came toward Jesus.*
>
> *But when he noticed the strong wind, he became frightened, and, beginning to sink, he cried out, "Lord, save me!"*
>
> *Jesus immediately reached out his hand and caught him, saying to him, "You of little faith, why did you doubt?"*
>
> *When they got into the boat, the wind ceased. And those in the boat worshiped him, saying, "Truly you are the Son of God." (Matthew 14:28-32)*

This is another story of Jesus rescuing his disciples and coming to their aid when they are overwhelmed. The disciples are understandably terrified when they see someone walking on the sea towards them, but when Jesus speaks to them, Peter is ready to believe.

If this is really Jesus, then he will be safer out on the sea with him than inside the boat. Jesus doesn't laugh at his request. He simply says, "Come." And so Peter does, and I don't know how many steps he took or whether he had time to appreciate the experience, but when he "noticed the strong wind, he became frightened."

Reflect

If you were crossing the sea with the disciples, where would you have been? In the boat? Out on the waves with Jesus?

Overflowing Truth

Every time I read this passage, I am reminded of the importance of being focused on Jesus. Whether I am overwhelmed by difficulties or stepping out into a new experience, I need to keep my eyes on him.

> *Hear, O Lord, when I cry aloud;*
> *be gracious to me and answer me!*
> ***"Come," my heart says, "seek his face!"***
> ***Your face, Lord, do I seek.*** *(Psalm 27:7–8)*
> *I sought the Lord, and he answered me*
> *and delivered me from all my fears.*
> ***Look to him, and be radiant,***
> ***so your faces shall never be ashamed.*** *(Psalm 34:4–5)*
> *The Lord is faithful in all his words*
> *and gracious in all his deeds.*
> ***The Lord upholds all who are falling***
> ***and raises up all who are bowed down.*** *(Psalm 145:13–14)*
> *I don't mean to say that I have already achieved these things*
> *or that I have already reached perfection.*
> ***But I press on to possess***
> ***that perfection for which Christ Jesus first possessed me.***
> *No, dear brothers and sisters, I have not achieved it,*
> *but I focus on this one thing:*
> *Forgetting the past and looking forward to what lies ahead,*
> ***I press on to reach the end of the race and receive the heavenly prize***
> ***for which God, through Christ Jesus, is calling us.*** *(Philippians 3:12–14 NLT)*

Reflect

What does it mean to you, in practical terms, to focus on Jesus? What actions does this focus involve?

Shipwrecked, Bitten by a Snake, & Other Adventures

The last verses in the Scriptures we just read are from the book of Philippians. The Apostle Paul wrote them, expressing his single-minded focus on Jesus. It seems appropriate to look at a story from his life today.

Our story begins with Paul as a prisoner on a ship bound for Rome. Paul is aware that trouble lies ahead for this ship, and he warns the crew several times.

> *...Paul then stood up among them and said, "Men, you should have listened to me and not have set sail from Crete and thereby avoided this damage and loss. I urge you now to keep up your courage, for there will be no loss of life among you, but only of the ship. For last night there stood by me an angel of the God to whom I belong and whom I worship, and he said, 'Do not be afraid, Paul; you must stand before the emperor, and, indeed, God has granted safety to all those who are sailing with you.' So keep up your courage, men, for I have faith in God that it will be exactly as I have been told. But we will have to run aground on some island." (Acts 27:21-26)*

Unsurprisingly, the ship does run aground, and Paul is in for a wild series of adventures.

> *But striking a reef, they ran the ship aground; the bow stuck and remained immovable, but the stern was being broken up by the force of the waves. The soldiers' plan was to kill the prisoners, so that none might swim away and escape; but the centurion, wishing to save Paul, kept them from carrying out their plan. He ordered those who could swim to jump overboard first and make for the land and the rest to follow, some on planks and others on pieces of the ship. And so it was that all were brought safely to land.*
>
> *After we had reached safety, we then learned that the island was called Malta. The local people showed us unusual kindness. Since it had begun to rain and was cold, they kindled a fire and welcomed all of us around it. Paul had gathered a bundle of brushwood and was putting it on the fire when a viper, driven out by the heat, fastened itself on his hand. When the local people saw the creature hanging from his hand, they said to one another, "This man must be a murderer; though he has escaped from the sea, Justice has not allowed him to live." He, however, shook off the creature into the fire and suffered no harm. They were expecting him to swell up or drop dead, but after they had waited a long time and saw that nothing unusual had happened to him, they changed their minds and began to say that he was a god.*
>
> *Now in the vicinity of that place were lands belonging to the leading man of the island, named Publius, who received us and entertained us hospitably for three days. It so happened that the father of Publius lay sick in bed with fever and dysentery. Paul visited him and cured him by praying and putting his hands on him. After this happened, the rest of the people on the island who had diseases also came and were cured. They bestowed many honors on us, and when we were about to sail, they put on board all the provisions we needed. (Acts 27:41-28:10)*

There is a lot of drama in this segment of Scripture! Notice that the writer occasionally uses the word "we." Luke, the author of Acts, is along for the ride on this journey with Paul.

The soldiers want to kill all the prisoners, but the centurion changes their minds. Everyone swims or floats to shore clinging to whatever floating bits of the boat they can find. The local people are kind, building a fire and helping everyone warm up and dry out.

But the story isn't over. Paul helps to gather wood for the fire, and gets bitten by a viper! The people immediately decide he must be a murderer, then change their minds and declare that he is a god. Paul just keeps on keeping on, praying and healing, and eventually sailing away, bound for Rome, and ultimately, martyrdom.

Reflect

How would you describe Paul's attitude in these Scriptures?

Hebrews 12:1-3 presents the attitude of focusing on Jesus in detail. We are looking at it in two versions. Notice how Jesus is described (in bold print), the choice Jesus made, and what effect considering Jesus will have on our lives.

> *Therefore, since we are surrounded by so great a cloud of witnesses,*
> *let us also lay aside every weight and the sin that clings so closely,*
> *and let us run with perseverance the race that is set before us,*
> *looking to* ***Jesus, the pioneer and perfecter of faith,***
> *who for the sake of the joy that was set before him endured the cross,*
> *disregarding its shame, and has taken his seat at the right hand of the throne of God.*
> *Consider him who endured such hostility against himself from sinners,*
> *so that you may not grow weary in your souls or lose heart.*
> *(Hebrews 12:1-3, emphasis added)*
> *Therefore, since we are surrounded by such a huge crowd of witnesses to the life of faith,*
> *let us strip off every weight that slows us down, especially the sin that so easily trips us up.*
> *And let us run with endurance the race God has set before us.*
> *We do this by keeping our eyes on* ***Jesus, the champion who initiates and perfects our faith.***
> *Because of the joy awaiting him, he endured the cross, disregarding its shame.*
> *Now he is seated in the place of honor beside God's throne.*
> *Think of all the hostility he endured from sinful people;*
> *then you won't become weary and give up. (Hebrews 12:1-3 NLT, emphasis added)*

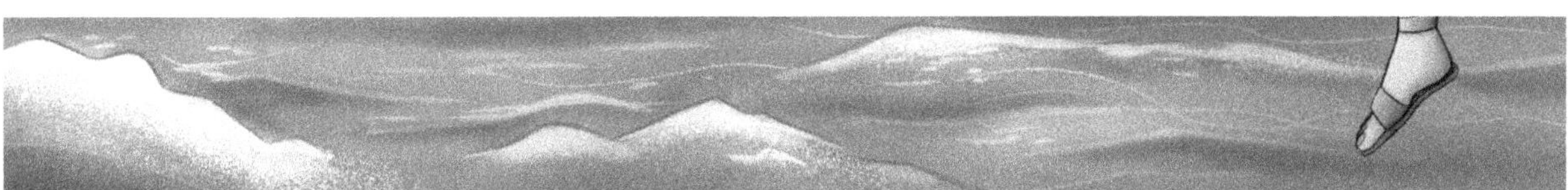

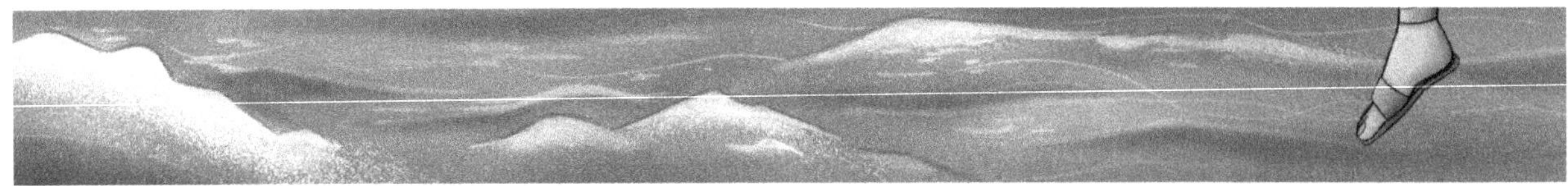

The following psalm will remind you of the way God rescued the Israelites at the Red Sea in the book of Exodus. I placed it in this chapter because it describes God's power over the waves and his path through the mighty waters. When the disciples saw Jesus displaying this same power, it was a big clue to Jesus' identity.

Your way, O God, is holy.
What god is so great as our God?
You are the God who works wonders;
you have displayed your might among the peoples.
With your strong arm you redeemed your people,
the descendants of Jacob and Joseph. Selah
When the waters saw you, O God,
when the waters saw you, they were afraid;
the very deep trembled.
The clouds poured out water;
the skies thundered;
your arrows flashed on every side.
The crash of your thunder was in the whirlwind;
your lightnings lit up the world;
the earth trembled and shook.
Your way was through the sea,
your path through the mighty waters,
yet your footprints were unseen.
You led your people like a flock
by the hand of Moses and Aaron. *(Psalm 77:11–20)*

Reflect

Which phrases in the psalm caught your attention?

Closing Prayer

By the word of the Lord the heavens were made
and all their host by the breath of his mouth.
He gathered the waters of the sea as in a bottle;
he put the deeps in storehouses.
Let all the earth fear the Lord;
let all the inhabitants of the world stand in awe of him.
(Psalm 33:6–8)

~Notes~

Beside Still Waters

a personal time of meditation and prayer

Read Matthew 14 to see the context of our Gospel Focus story. You may want to use a meditation method from page 100 or 101 as you meditate on this chapter or the verses below.

As you revisit the following verses, look for phrases you can use in prayer or thanksgiving.

> *Therefore, since we are surrounded by so great a cloud of witnesses,*
> *let us also lay aside every weight and the sin that clings so closely,*
> *and let us run with perseverance the race that is set before us,*
> *looking to* ***Jesus, the pioneer and perfecter of faith,***
> *who for the sake of the joy that was set before him endured the cross,*
> *disregarding its shame, and has taken his seat at the right hand of the throne of God.*
> *Consider him who endured such hostility against himself from sinners,*
> *so that you may not grow weary in your souls or lose heart.*
> *(Hebrews 12:1–3, emphasis added)*
> *Therefore, since we are surrounded by such a huge crowd of witnesses to the life of faith,*
> *let us strip off every weight that slows us down, especially the sin that so easily trips us up.*
> *And let us run with endurance the race God has set before us.*
> *We do this by keeping our eyes on* ***Jesus, the champion who initiates and perfects our faith.***
> *Because of the joy awaiting him, he endured the cross, disregarding its shame.*
> *Now he is seated in the place of honor beside God's throne.*
> *Think of all the hostility he endured from sinful people;*
> *then you won't become weary and give up. (Hebrews 12:1–3 NLT, emphasis added)*

~Notes~

Chapter 10: Fishing for Tax Money

Reflect

Think of a small animal or tiny object in nature that you find fascinating.

Gospel Focus

After several chapters of raging storms and dramatic healings, we turn to a short story of a small need that is met in an unusual way.

> *When they reached Capernaum, the collectors of the temple tax came to Peter and said, "Does your teacher not pay the temple tax?"*
> *He said, "Yes, he does."*
> *And when he came home, Jesus spoke of it first, asking, "What do you think, Simon? From whom do kings of the earth take toll or tribute? From their children or from others?"*
> *When Peter said, "From others," Jesus said to him, "Then the children are free. However, so that we do not give offense to them, go to the sea and cast a hook; take the first fish that comes up, and when you open its mouth you will find a coin; take that and give it to them for you and me." (Matthew 17:24-27)*

Every Jewish male was required to pay a yearly tax of one coin (specifically a *drachma*, about one day's wage) to support the temple's upkeep. However, there were groups of people who refused to pay because they felt they were exempt.[1] These temple tax collectors may have been wondering if Jesus would take a side on the issue. Jesus certainly had strong opinions about various aspects of the religious system. They may have been hoping to hear a fiery speech that they could quote to their leaders as proof that Jesus was a troublemaker.

Peter might be surprised that Jesus didn't want to offend people about this issue. I am sure that Peter has heard Jesus say many things that offended many people!

Jesus speaks of kings who do not tax their children, and the message is clear: Jesus, as the Son of God, shouldn't have to pay this temple tax. But Jesus doesn't use this opportunity to make a big theological statement. Instead, he provides the funds in a unique way. As a man who earned his livelihood by fishing, Peter may be a little amused by this.

In the original Greek, the word for the coin in the fish is *statēr,* a coin worth two *drachma.* Thus, this little fishing trip would provide the yearly tax payment for both Jesus and Peter.

Reflect

Why do you think Jesus chose to stay silent on this issue and not make a big deal about it?

Scholar Michael Card suggests that perhaps Jesus just wanted a quiet evening with his friends.[2] They were more valuable to him than yet another argument with the religious leaders. Whatever the reason, Jesus gave us an example of choosing not to speak up on every subject.

I have always loved this story. It reminds me that Jesus cares about the small details. As we read the stories of dramatic miracles in the Bible, it is easy to forget that the Lord cares for each of us and our daily problems.

Overflowing Truth

God cares about you, every day, every moment of the day, in summer and winter, good times and bad. How does this truth change your life?

Have you ever prayed about finding a small lost item? Or does this seem too trivial to bother God about?

As I looked for Scriptures to express God's personal care for us, I thought of Psalm 23. Shepherds must care for their flock as a whole, but they also have to be aware of each individual animal. The Lord our shepherd knows and cares about our needs, whether we are resting beside still waters or walking through dark valleys. His goodness and mercy follow us every day of our lives. None of our worries and concerns are too small to bring to the Lord in prayer. As you read this psalm (in two versions), look for the types of situations in which the shepherd cares for his sheep.

> *The Lord is my shepherd; I shall not want.*
> ***He makes me lie down in green pastures;***
> *he leads me beside still waters; he restores my soul.*
> ***He leads me in right paths for his name's sake.***
> *Even though I walk through the darkest valley,*
> ***I fear no evil, for you are with me;***
> *your rod and your staff, they comfort me.*
> ***You prepare a table before me in the presence of my enemies;***
> *you anoint my head with oil; my cup overflows.*
> ***Surely goodness and mercy shall follow me***
> *all the days of my life,*
> ***and I shall dwell in the house of the Lord***
> *my whole life long. (Psalm 23)*

The Lord is my shepherd;
I have all that I need.
He lets me rest in green meadows;
he leads me beside peaceful streams.
He renews my strength.
He guides me along right paths,
bringing honor to his name.
Even when I walk through the darkest valley,
I will not be afraid, for you are close beside me.
Your rod and your staff protect and comfort me.
You prepare a feast for me in the presence of my enemies.
You honor me by anointing my head with oil.
My cup overflows with blessings.
Surely your goodness and unfailing love
will pursue me all the days of my life,
and I will live in the house of the Lord forever. *(Psalm 23 NLT)*

Reflect

How would you express the needs that the Shepherd meets in this psalm? What kind of situations is the author experiencing?

What stories from the Scriptures would you add to illustrate the truth of God's care for us in the large events as well as the small issues of our lives?

A Floating Ax

I chose a very short story from the Old Testament as our supplementary Scripture in this chapter.

> *Now the company of prophets said to Elisha, "As you see, the place where we live under your charge is too small for us. Let us go to the Jordan, and let us collect logs there, one for each of us, and build a place there for us to live."*
> *He answered, "Do so."*
> *Then one of them said, "Please come with your servants."*
> *And he answered, "I will." So he went with them. When they came to the Jordan, they cut down trees.*
> *But as one was felling a log, his ax head fell into the water; he cried out, "Alas, master! It was borrowed."*
> *Then the man of God said, "Where did it fall?" When he showed him the place, he cut off a stick and threw it in there and made the iron float. He said, "Pick it up." So he reached out his hand and took it.* (2 Kings 6:1-7)

Elisha is one of the great Old Testament prophets. With God's help, he performs impressive miracles and powerfully proclaims God's message. In this brief event, we see him visiting a building site and coming to the aid of a man who lost an ax. I am sure that tools such as this had a larger value in the ancient world than they do today, but even so, this is a small miracle in comparison to raising the dead or rescuing a family from poverty. This story speaks to me of God's care for each of us in our everyday activities.

Reflect

As you read these Scriptures, consider what they tell you about prayer, and also about how God values you.

> *Is there anyone among you who,*
> *if your child asked for bread, would give a stone?*
> ***Or if the child asked for a fish, would give a snake?***
> *If you, then, who are evil,*
> *know how to give good gifts to your children,*
> ***how much more will your Father in heaven give good things***
> ***to those who ask him!*** *(Matthew 7:9-11)*
> *Are not five sparrows sold for two pennies?*
> *Yet not one of them is forgotten in God's sight.*
> ***But even the hairs of your head are all numbered.***
> ***Do not be afraid; you are of more value than many sparrows.*** *(Luke 12:6-7)*
> *Do not be anxious about anything, but in everything by prayer*
> *and supplication with thanksgiving*
> ***let your requests be made known to God.***
> *And the peace of God, which surpasses all understanding,*

will guard your hearts and your minds in Christ Jesus. *(Philippians 4:6–7)*
For the Lord is a great God and a great King above all gods.
In his hand are the depths of the earth;
the heights of the mountains are his also.
The sea is his, for he made it,
and the dry land, which his hands have formed.
O come, let us worship and bow down;
let us kneel before the Lord, our Maker!
For he is our God,
and we are the people of his pasture
and the sheep of his hand. *(Psalm 95:3–7)*
O Lord, you have searched me and known me.
You know when I sit down and when I rise up;
you discern my thoughts from far away.
You search out my path and my lying down
and are acquainted with all my ways. *(Psalm 139:1–3)*

Reflect

What did the preceding Scriptures tell you about prayer?

What did the Scriptures tell you about God's care of you?

Closing Prayer

Heavenly Father,
I come to you today in confident faith
sharing my concerns
my longings
my heart
because I know that you
mighty Creator God
care about every detail
of your creation
including me.

~Notes~

Beside Still Waters

a personal time of meditation and prayer

Read Matthew 17 to put the Gospel story of this chapter into context, using any meditation method you choose.

Are there any small things that are giving you stress today? Maybe a combination of little things has led to a great big burden of stress. Talk to the Lord about this.

Look back at the other Scriptures quoted in this chapter. Look for phrases you can use in a prayer of thanksgiving.

Surely goodness and mercy shall follow me
all the days of my life,
and I shall dwell in the house of the Lord
my whole life long. (Psalm 23)

~Notes~

Chapter 11:
A Basin of Water & an Example

Reflect

Have you ever received assistance from a friend or acquaintance during a humbling situation? Did that change your relationship with that person?

Gospel Focus

In John 13, as he gathers his disciples for a Passover Feast, Jesus knows that his death is approaching. He knows that he will soon return to the Father. Matthew, Mark, and Luke tell us of Jesus giving his disciples the vivid symbol of his sacrifice in the bread and the wine of the Last Supper at this time. But in the book of John, he demonstrates his love and his sacrifice in a different way.

At some time during this Passover Feast, the disciples quarrel over who is the greatest of them (Luke 22:24). Judas, trying to take his own path to power, will betray Jesus in a few hours, but he is still in the room when Jesus fills a basin with water and startles everyone with his act of service.

> *Jesus, knowing that the Father had given all things into his hands and that he had come from God and was going to God, got up from supper, took off his outer robe, and tied a towel around himself. Then he poured water into a basin and began to wash the disciples' feet and to wipe them with the towel that was tied around him. (John 13:3-5)*

Washing your feet was a daily routine in this land of dusty roads and foot travel. When you entered the home of a friend, they would often offer a small tub of water for you to wash your own feet. But the act of washing your feet–actually kneeling in front of you and unbuckling your sandals and washing away the dirt–this was the work of the lowest servant in the house.

Jesus, about to die a criminal's death, shows his humility by washing the feet of his disciples. This was a truly shocking action in their culture. You can imagine Peter, outspoken as always, watching Jesus approaching with a towel and a basin of water, and simply telling Jesus what he thought of this.

Reflect

What do you think you might have felt or said if you saw Jesus washing the feet of your friends, and now approaching you?

> *He came to Simon Peter, who said to him, "Lord, are you going to wash my feet?"*
> *Jesus answered, "You do not know now what I am doing, but later you will understand."*
> *Peter said to him, "You will never wash my feet."*
> *Jesus answered, "Unless I wash you, you have no share with me."*
> *Simon Peter said to him, "Lord, not my feet only but also my hands and my head!"*
> *Jesus said to him, "One who has bathed does not need to wash, except for the feet, but is entirely clean. And you are clean, though not all of you." For he knew who was to betray him; for this reason he said, "Not all of you are clean." (John 13:6–11)*

Peter, at first appalled by Jesus' actions, is now ready to jump in with both feet. But Jesus says this isn't necessary. My study Bible uses the word "pre-enactment" here to express what Jesus is doing.[1] Those who trust him will be washed clean from sin and guilt by his sacrifice on the cross. In the scene we just read, that sacrifice is in the near future, but Jesus is giving them a small pre-enactment of what will happen. He is also vividly illustrating the attitude they will need to cultivate when they work together as the earliest members of the Church.

> *After he had washed their feet, had put on his robe, and had reclined again, he said to them, "Do you know what I have done to you? You call me Teacher and Lord, and you are right, for that is what I am. So if I, your Lord and Teacher, have washed your feet, you also ought to wash one another's feet. For I have set you an example, that you also should do as I have done to you." (John 13:12–15)*

Reflect

What did this story tell you about Jesus' attitude and character?

Why do you think Jesus chose to give his disciples this very visual lesson at their last dinner before his crucifixion?

Overflowing Truth

The humility of Jesus gives us an example to follow. As you read the following Scripture, notice the instructions the author (Paul) is giving his readers. Also, take note of how Jesus is described. We are reading this passage from two versions of the Bible.

> *If, then, there is any comfort in Christ, any consolation from love,*
> ***any partnership in the Spirit, any tender affection and sympathy,***
> *make my joy complete: be of the same mind, having the same love,*
> ***being in full accord and of one mind.***
> *Do nothing from selfish ambition or empty conceit,*
> ***but in humility regard others as better than yourselves.***
> *Let each of you look not to your own interests but to the interests of others.*

Let the same mind be in you that was in Christ Jesus,
who, though he existed in the form of God,
did not regard equality with God as something to be grasped,
but emptied himself, taking the form of a slave, assuming human likeness.
And being found in appearance as a human, he humbled himself
and became obedient to the point of death—even death on a cross.
Therefore God exalted him even more highly
and gave him the name that is above every other name,
so that at the name given to Jesus every knee should bend,
in heaven and on earth and under the earth,
and every tongue should confess that Jesus Christ is Lord,
to the glory of God the Father. (Philippians 2:1-11)
Is there any encouragement from belonging to Christ?
Any comfort from his love? Any fellowship together in the Spirit?
Are your hearts tender and compassionate? Then make me truly happy
by agreeing wholeheartedly with each other, loving one another,
and working together with one mind and purpose.
Don't be selfish; don't try to impress others.
Be humble, thinking of others as better than yourselves.
Don't look out only for your own interests, but take an interest in others, too.
You must have the same attitude that Christ Jesus had.
Though he was God,
he did not think of equality with God as something to cling to.
Instead, he gave up his divine privileges;
he took the humble position of a slave and was born as a human being.
When he appeared in human form, he humbled himself in obedience to God
and died a criminal's death on a cross.
Therefore, God elevated him to the place of highest honor
and gave him the name above all other names,
that at the name of Jesus every knee should bow,
in heaven and on earth and under the earth,
and every tongue declare that Jesus Christ is Lord,
to the glory of God the Father. *(Philippians 2:1-11 NLT)*

Reflect

What did this passage tell you about Jesus and his attitude?

What instructions did the passage give you about living the Christian life?

Healing & Humility At The Jordan

Jesus called his disciples to a life of humility, a life poured out in service to others. Sometimes an attitude of humility is necessary for a healing experience, as Naaman found out in 2 Kings.

> *Naaman, commander of the army of the king of Aram, was a great man and in high favor with his master because by him the Lord had given victory to Aram. The man, though a mighty warrior, suffered from a skin disease. Now the Arameans on one of their raids had taken a young girl captive from the land of Israel, and she served Naaman's wife. She said to her mistress, "If only my lord were with the prophet who is in Samaria! He would cure him of his skin disease." (2 Kings 5:1-3)*

This story has always fascinated me. Here is a young girl who has been snatched away from her home and forced into slavery. Yet, within her enslaved position, she shares the truth she knows about a prophet of God.

> *So Naaman went in and told his lord just what the girl from the land of Israel had said. And the king of Aram said, "Go, then, and I will send along a letter to the king of Israel." He went, taking with him ten talents of silver, six thousand shekels of gold, and ten sets of garments. He brought the letter to the king of Israel, which read, "When this letter reaches you, know that I have sent to you my servant Naaman, that you may cure him of his skin disease." When the king of Israel read the letter, he tore his clothes and said, "Am I God, to give death or life, that this man sends word to me to cure a man of his skin disease? Just look and see how he is trying to pick a quarrel with me." (2 Kings 5:4-7)*

Naaman, a man of power and position, goes to Israel, but he goes to the king, not to the prophet. The king is shocked and terrified, knowing that he can do nothing to help. He is afraid that his inability will lead to an attack by Naaman and his army.

> *But when Elisha the man of God heard that the king of Israel had torn his clothes, he sent a message to the king, "Why have you torn your clothes? Let him come to me, that he may learn that there is a prophet in Israel."*
>
> *So Naaman came with his horses and chariots and halted at the entrance of Elisha's house. Elisha sent a messenger to him, saying, "Go, wash in the Jordan seven times, and your flesh shall be restored, and you shall be clean."*
>
> *But Naaman became angry and went away, saying, "I thought that for me he would surely come out and stand and call on the name of the Lord his God and would wave his hand over the spot and cure the skin disease! Are not Abana and Pharpar, the rivers of Damascus, better than all the waters of Israel? Could I*

not wash in them and be clean?" He turned and went away in a rage. (2 Kings 5:9-12)

Naaman is expecting a great spectacle, a healing miracle that not only erases his disease, but shows him off as a great man. He is disgusted at the whole idea of bathing in the Jordan.

But his servants approached and said to him, "Father, if the prophet had commanded you to do something difficult, would you not have done it? How much more, when all he said to you was, 'Wash, and be clean'?" So he went down and immersed himself seven times in the Jordan, according to the word of the man of God; his flesh was restored like the flesh of a young boy, and he was clean. (2 Kings 5:13-14)

Naaman's servants suggest that he has nothing to lose by trying out the prophet's advice. And so he approches this river that he despises, and bathes in it. (I wonder how many people of Israel were watching this powerful foreign man dunk himself in the river Jordan.)

Then he returned to the man of God, he and all his company; he came and stood before him and said, "Now I know that there is no God in all the earth except in Israel; please accept a present from your servant."
But he said, "As the Lord lives, whom I serve, I will accept nothing!" He urged him to accept, but he refused. (2 Kings 5:15-16)

Elisha, a humble man himself, refuses to be paid for a miracle has been accomplished by God's power.

Reflect

What are your reactions to this story? How would you describe

- the servant girl
- Naaman
- Elisha

Closing Prayer

Good and upright is the Lord;
therefore he instructs sinners in the way.
He leads the humble in what is right
and teaches the humble his way.
All the paths of the Lord
are steadfast love and faithfulness,
for those who keep his covenant
and his decrees. (Psalm 25:8-10)

~Notes~

Beside Still Waters

a personal time of meditation and prayer

Choose one of these passages for your meditation today:
John 13 (This could be a great chapter to use the Imagine the Scene meditation method.)
Philippians 2:1-11 (Listen & Respond, Colorful Meditation, or Comparing Translations are all good meditation methods for this selection.)

Can you think of other events in the Gospels that show Jesus' humility?

Close your time with prayer.

Teach me good judgment and knowledge,
for I believe in your commandments.
Before I was humbled I went astray,
but now I keep your word.
You are good and do good;
teach me your statutes. (Psalm 119:66-68)

~Notes~

Chapter 12: Breakfast on the Beach

Reflect

When was the last time you had a picnic meal? Where were you?

Gospel Focus

Today we are reading about a picnic breakfast after the Resurrection of Jesus.

> *After these things Jesus showed himself again to the disciples by the Sea of Tiberias, and he showed himself in this way. Gathered there together were Simon Peter, Thomas called the Twin, Nathanael of Cana in Galilee, the sons of Zebedee, and two others of his disciples. Simon Peter said to them, "I am going fishing."*
>
> *They said to him, "We will go with you." (John 21:1-3)*

The Sea of Tiberias is another name for the Sea of Galilee. Previously, Jesus had promised his disciples that he would meet them in Galilee. (Matthew 28:10)

> *They went out and got into the boat, but that night they caught nothing. Just after daybreak, Jesus stood on the beach, but the disciples did not know that it was Jesus. Jesus said to them, "Children, you have no fish, have you?"*
>
> *They answered him, "No."*
>
> *He said to them, "Cast the net to the right side of the boat, and you will find some." So they cast it, and now they were not able to haul it in because there were so many fish.*
>
> *That disciple whom Jesus loved said to Peter, "It is the Lord!" When Simon Peter heard that it was the Lord, he put on his outer garment, for he had taken it off, and jumped into the sea. But the other disciples came in the boat, dragging the net full of fish, for they were not far from the land, only about a hundred yards off. (John 21:4-8)*

In a scene that must remind the men of the day Jesus called them to follow him, they bring in a huge catch of fish after a long fruitless night. John is the first to realize that the man on the shore is Jesus. Peter jumps into the sea and rushes to Jesus.

This is not the first time Peter has seen the risen Lord (see Luke 24:34). I presume that Jesus and Peter have talked about Peter's denial, and that Peter has been assured of his forgiveness, because there is no uncertainty in Peter's actions here. This is a man who sees his dearest friend, and is anxious to be near him again.

> *When they had gone ashore, they saw a charcoal fire there, with fish on it, and bread. Jesus said to them, "Bring some of the fish that you have just caught." So Simon Peter went aboard and hauled the net ashore, full of large fish, a hundred fifty-three of them, and*

though there were so many, the net was not torn. Jesus said to them, "Come and have breakfast."

Now none of the disciples dared to ask him, "Who are you?" because they knew it was the Lord. Jesus came and took the bread and gave it to them and did the same with the fish. This was now the third time that Jesus appeared to the disciples after he was raised from the dead. (John 21:9–14)

This is one of my favorite stories of Jesus. He could have come to them in all kinds of miraculous and astounding ways, but he chose to make a simple breakfast to share with his friends.

When they had finished breakfast, Jesus said to Simon Peter, "Simon son of John, do you love me more than these?"

He said to him, "Yes, Lord; you know that I love you."

Jesus said to him, "Feed my lambs." A second time he said to him, "Simon son of John, do you love me?"

He said to him, "Yes, Lord; you know that I love you."

Jesus said to him, "Tend my sheep." He said to him the third time, "Simon son of John, do you love me?"

Peter felt hurt because he said to him the third time, "Do you love me?" And he said to him, "Lord, you know everything; you know that I love you."

Jesus said to him, "Feed my sheep. (John 21:15–17)

Jesus has planned a prominent role for Peter in the early church, and I think this scene shows him preparing Peter for it. Just as Peter denied Jesus three times, so Jesus gives him three opportunities to proclaim his love for him. Jesus also gives him an assignment, and repeats it three times.

Overflowing Truth

In this beautiful story, I see three overflowing truths about interacting with Jesus. First, I see Jesus meeting his friends in everyday moments. They are doing what they know (fishing), facing a common frustration (not catching anything) when Jesus appears and gives them (in addition to the big catch of fish) a simple breakfast. We've spent quite a few weeks seeing Jesus meeting people in various ways, some of them quite miraculous. I hope we haven't forgotten that we can meet him in the everyday routines of our lives. We can notice his presence in our daily prayers, in a nourishing meal, or in a sunset we just happen to glimpse.

...Remember, I am with you always, to the end of the age. (Matthew 28:20)

Secondly, I see that the disciples met Jesus in an unexpected way. They had always been longing for a military Messiah. I am sure they were hoping that the risen Jesus would appear in some spectacular way, driving out the Romans and setting up his kingdom on earth, with the disciples as his powerful representatives. Instead, Jesus cooked their breakfast. This is such a good reminder to us. Sometimes when we are hoping that the Lord will answer our prayers in a specific way, we get so focused on our plans that we miss him leading us in a different direction.

"My thoughts are nothing like your thoughts," says the Lord.
"And my ways are far beyond anything you could imagine." (Isaiah 55:8 NLT)

And thirdly, I see what happens when you meet Jesus after you have failed him. Peter seems to already know that Jesus has forgiven him, but that's not the end of the story. Jesus also has work for Peter to do. He does not need to spend the rest of his life bemoaning his big mistake; he is called to move on to a new chapter.

Oh, what joy for those whose disobedience is forgiven,
whose sins are put out of sight. (Romans 4:7 NLT)

Peter certainly did move forward. The book of Acts shows Peter in several pivotal moments, fearlessly proclaiming the gospel of Jesus Christ. Later, in the book of I Peter, he gives advice to other Christian leaders:

...Tend the flock of God that is in your charge,
exercising the oversight, not under compulsion but willingly,
as God would have you do it, not for sordid gain but eagerly.
Do not lord it over those in your charge, but be examples to the flock.
And when the chief shepherd appears,
you will win the crown of glory that never fades away. (I Peter 5:2-4)

Reflect

What encouraging truths did you see in the story of breakfast on the beach?

The Spring of the Water of Life

The Scripture I chose to accompany the portrait of breakfast on the beach is a Scripture that shows our future with God at the spring of the water of life.

"See, the home of God is among mortals.
He will dwell with them;
they will be his peoples,
and God himself will be with them and be their God;
he will wipe every tear from their eyes.
Death will be no more;
mourning and crying and pain will be no more,
for the first things have passed away."
And the one who was seated on the throne said, "See, I am making all things new."

Also he said, "Write this, for these words are trustworthy and true."
Then he said to me, "It is done! I am the Alpha and the Omega, the Beginning and the End.
To the thirsty I will give water as a gift from the spring of the water of life.
(Revelation 21:3-6)
Then the angel showed me the river of the water of life, bright as crystal,
flowing from the throne of God and of the Lamb
through the middle of the street of the city.
On either side of the river is the tree of life with its twelve kinds of fruit,
producing its fruit each month, and the leaves of the tree are for the healing of the nations.
Nothing accursed will be found there any more.
But the throne of God and of the Lamb will be in it,
and his servants will worship him;
they will see his face, and his name will be on their foreheads.
And there will be no more night; they need no light of lamp or sun,
for the Lord God will be their light, and they will reign forever and ever.
(Revelation 22:1-5)

Here we have a description of the future that awaits us: a bright and peaceful home where everything is new. And flowing through this bright future is the river of the water of life. It is a land where our goblets will never be empty, we will never be threatened by storms or drought or disease, and we will see the face of our Savior.

Reflect

What details in the Scriptures caught your attention? Which of them make you long for this future with God?

Take a quick glance back at our previous chapters. What has encouraged you in this study of *Rescue & Refreshment*?

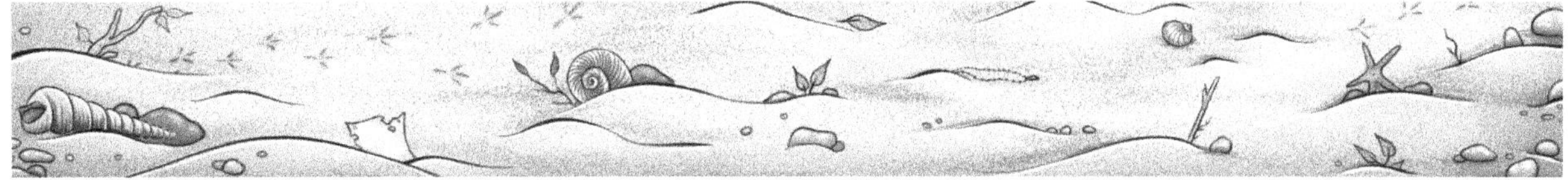

Is there something about the character of Jesus that you have learned (or been reminded of) in this study?

Which Bible character(s) did you admire or learn from in this study?

Closing Prayer

Your steadfast love, O Lord, extends to the heavens,
your faithfulness to the clouds.
Your righteousness is like the mighty mountains;
your judgments are like the great deep;
you save humans and animals alike, O Lord.
How precious is your steadfast love, O God!
All people may take refuge in the shadow of your wings.
They feast on the abundance of your house,
and you give them drink from the river of your delights.
For with you is the fountain of life;
in your light we see light. (Psalm 36:5–9)

~Notes~

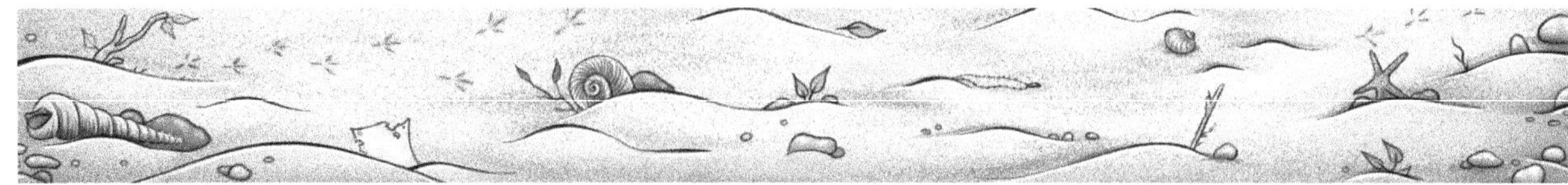

Beside Still Waters

a personal time of meditation and prayer

Read John 21, and use your favorite method of meditating on the text.

Take a few moments to consider the ideas of rescue and refreshment. Which of these words expresses the needs of your heart today? Talk to the Lord about your needs and his promises.

> *O God, you are my God; I seek you;*
> *my soul thirsts for you; my flesh faints for you,*
> *as in a dry and weary land where there is no water. (Psalm 63:1)*
> *... Let anyone who is thirsty come to me,*
> *and let the one who believes in me drink.*
> *As the scripture has said, "Out of the believer's heart*
> *shall flow rivers of living water." (John 7:37–38)*

~Notes~

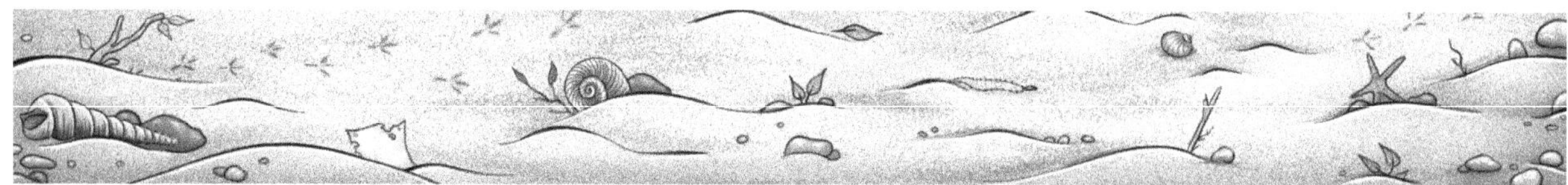

Appendix

Meditation Methods & Suggestions

When I use the word "meditation" in this study, I mean the act of spending time in the Scriptures and dwelling on them.

I find that the easiest way to do this is to ask myself questions about what I just read. One of the benefits of choosing a method to follow is that it allows me to easily refocus when I get distracted.

Below you will find several methods of meditation. You might want to try a different method every week until you find your favorite.

The most important first step in whatever method you use is to take a moment and ask God to guide your time with him, to focus your mind, and quiet your heart.

1. Focus on Jesus

Ask yourself these questions about the Scriptures you just read.

- What did this story tell you about Jesus' character?
- What did this story tell you about how Jesus interacts with people?
- After reading this story, how will you respond to Jesus?

2. Colorful Meditation

Grab a few colored pens or pencils, and use them while you pray. You might write a phrase or two in big colorful letters, and doodle around them. Or you could draw stick figures to illustrate the scene. Maybe you just want to use colors and shapes to express your mood during prayer.

This can be a valuable meditation method for those who are easily distracted, because it keeps your hands busy and your mind focused while you spend more time with God's Word.[1]

3. Listen & Respond

You will want to read the whole chapter you are using today, and then choose a section of just 5 or 6 verses within the chapter. Use that smaller section as you spend time with the following questions. Reread your chosen section at least three times.

- What word or phrase caught your attention when you read the Scripture today?
- Why is this word or phrase relevant to you right now?
- Respond to the Scriptures. What do you want to talk to Jesus about today? This might be a praise or a prayer.

4. Imagine the Scene

This is an especially thought-provoking method to use with the stories in the Gospels. It is easy: just think through your five senses, one at a time, and imagine what you might be experiencing if you were present in the scene you just read. Consider which character you identify with most, and whether you would act as that character did.

5. Comparing Translations

There are many websites that will allow you to do this if you do not have several translations of the printed Bible. I use biblegateway.com. I like to compare these versions of the Bible: NRSV, NLT, Amplified, and The Message.

6. Meditating on a Hymn

Poetry can speak to our hearts in a unique and personal way. If a study chapter brought a song to mind, look up the lyrics to that song. Listen to it or sing it, and write your favorite lyrics on your Notes page.

I have listed a few suggested hymns below. Do a web search for the lyrics (hymnary.org is a good source), listen to the song on your favorite streaming service, or look for a video on youtube.

Chapter 1: *Glorious Things Of Thee Are Spoken,* by John Newton
Chapter 2: *O The Deep, Deep Love Of Jesus,* by S. Trevor Francis
Chapter 3: *What A Friend We Have In Jesus*, by Joseph Medlicott Scriven
Chapter 4: *Jesus Calls Us,* by Cecil Frances Alexander
Chapter 5: *Satisfied*, by Clara Tear Williams
Chapter 6: *Open My Eyes*, by Clara H. Scott
Chapter 7: *Does Jesus Care*, by Frank E. Graeff
Chapter 8: *Victory In Jesus*, by E. M. Bartlett
Chapter 9: *Love Lifted Me*, by James Rowe
Chapter 10: *Day By Day*, by Carolina Sandell Berg
Chapter 11: *O Master Let Me Walk With Thee,* by Washington Gladden
Chapter 12: *More Love To Thee, O Christ*, by E. Prentiss

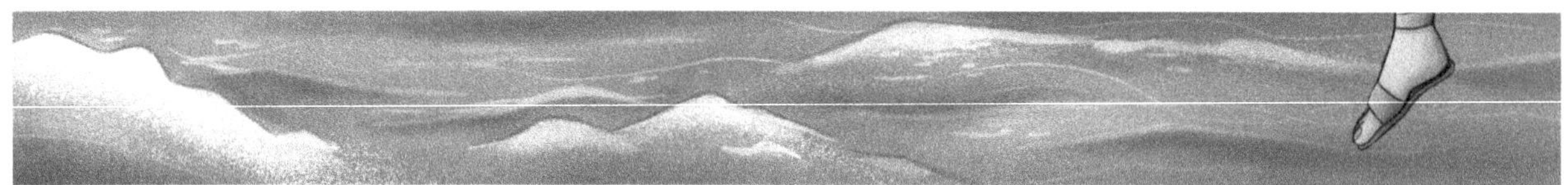

Footnotes

Chapter 1

1. Card, Michael, *John: The Gospel of Wisdom (*Downer's Grove, Illinois: Intervarsity Press, 2014), p. 12
2. Tverberg, Lois, at https://ourrabbijesus.com/articles/living-water/, accessed 7/25/2022
3. online concordance at https://www.blueletterbible.org/lexicon/g1372/kjv/tr/0-1/, accessed 7/25/2022
4. online concordance at https://www.blueletterbible.org/lexicon/h3444/kjv/wlc/0-1/, accesses 7/25/2022

Chapter 2

1. Card, Michael, *Luke: The Gospel of Amazement* (Downer's Grove, Illinois: Intervarsity Press, 2011), p. 59
2. Hall, Emily, at https://www.christianity.com/wiki/people/what-is-a-eunuch-in-the-bible-definition-and-examples.html accessed 7/25/2022

Chapter 3

Keener, Craig S. *IVP Bible Background Commentary: New Testament, Second Edition* (Downer's Grove, Illinois: Intervarsity Press, 2014), ebook

Chapter 5

1. Card, Michael, *John: The Gospel of Wisdom (*Downer's Grove, Illinois: Intervarsity Press, 2014), p. 69
2. Research on the Samaritan woman at margmowczko.com and https://scotmcknight.substack.com accessed 7/25/2022
3. Research on Lydia: https://margmowczko.com accessed 7/25/2022

Chapter 6

1. Card, Michael, *John: The Gospel of Wisdom* (Downer's Grove, Illinois: Intervarsity Press, 2014), p. 119
2. Wright, N. T., *John: 26 Studies for Individuals and Groups* (Downer's Grove, Illinois: Intervarsity Press, 2009), p. 38

Chapter 9

1. Walton, Dr. John, and Keener, Dr. Craig, editors, *NIV Cultural Backgrounds Study Bible* (Grand Rapids, Michigan: Zondervan, 2016), accessed online 7/25/2022

Chapter 10

1. Ibid., accessed 7/25/2022
2. Card, Michael, *Matthew: The Gospel of Identity* (Downer's Grove, Illinois: Intervarsity Press, 2013), p. 159

Chapter 11
1. Comfort, Phillip W. and Wolf, Matthew, editors, *NLT Parallel Study Bible*, (Carol Stream, Illinois: Tyndale House Publishers, Inc.), 2011, p.2012

Meditation Methods
1. Sybil Macbeth uses a method like this in her excellent book *Praying in Color: Drawing a New Path to God.*

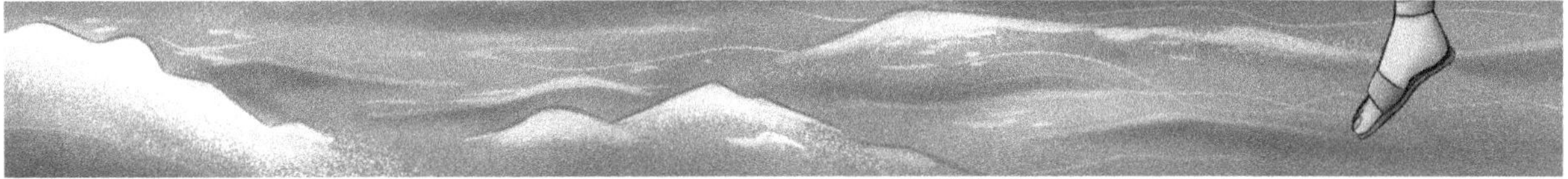

If you enjoyed this study, you might also appreciate
these other books by Ruth J. Leamy
at Amazon.com:

Luke: the Path of Peace
and
Beachcombing the Psalms

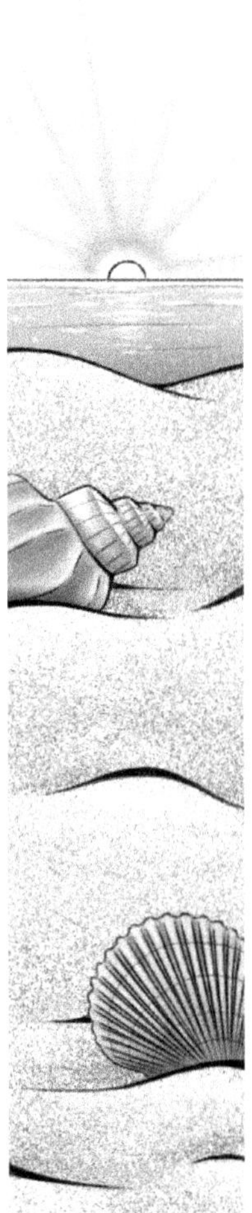

www.ingramcontent.com/pod-product-compliance
Lightning Source LLC
LaVergne TN
LVHW082248150826
845677LV00009B/1572

9798845618795